T. S. ELIOT AND EDUCATION

T. S. ELIOT
and
EDUCATION

G. H. BANTOCK

FABER AND FABER
London

First published in 1970
by Faber and Faber Limited
24 Russell Square London WC1
Printed in Great Britain by
Latimer Trend & Co Limited Plymouth

ISBN *(paper edition)* 0 571 09514 3
ISBN *(cloth edition)* 0 571 09435 x

Quotations from 'The Aims of Education' and
'American Literature and the American Langu-
age' are reprinted with the permission of
Faber and Faber Ltd. from *To Criticize the
Critic* by T. S. Eliot, copyright © 1965 by
Valerie Eliot.
Other quotations from the writings of T. S.
Eliot are reprinted with the permission of
Faber and Faber Ltd.

'. . . there should always be a few writers preoccupied in penetrating to the core of the matter, in trying to arrive at the truth and to set it forth, without too much hope, without ambition to alter the immediate course of affairs, and without being downcast or defeated when nothing appears to ensue.'

T. S. ELIOT

Preface

This book is intended primarily for students. T. S. Eliot was not a simple man, and his ideas are correspondingly complex. They can only be simplified to a limited extent; and it would be an ill service to either student or Eliot to pretend that their value does not, in part, depend on their very unconventionality. Where I have felt it to be helpful, then, I have not hesitated to repeat points in an attempt to make their relevance and meaning more apparent.

I am indebted to the firm of which he was a director, Faber & Faber, for permission to quote from his works extensively, for I have felt it important that the student should savour a good deal of Eliot at first hand. I am also very grateful to Mrs. T. S. Eliot for having corrected one or two biographical facts.

G. H. BANTOCK
University of Leicester

Contents

Introduction

T. S. Eliot made his name as a great poet and critic; and even given the fact that he wrote more on the subject of education than is commonly realized, it is still perhaps surprising that a whole, even if small, volume can be devoted to a consideration of his educational views. What qualifications, indeed, would a man of his particular interests and skills have that his comments on our system of schooling should be thought of any value? And what was it in the nature of his age that provoked him to devote even so much time to a subject normally the chosen field of specialists, who usually build on an extended period of practical experience increasingly technical considerations relating to very specific aspects of our educational system? It is true that Eliot was not totally without practical experience; furthermore, he received an extended academic education himself. But the direction of his later interests would seem to preclude his having any views worth the having on so technical a matter as our methods of bringing up the young.

It may be possible to assuage these doubts by examining both the extent of Eliot's direct experience of education and the nature of his interests and times which were likely to force on his attention, to some degree at least, a social phenomenon as important and as far-reaching as our educational system. Furthermore, the exercise of his craft as poet and critic—the particular nature of the life role he chose to assume—also had important implications for his educational theorizing, a consideration which will be discussed in the next chapter.

Eliot was born in St. Louis, Missouri in 1888, the seventh and youngest child. The family was of English origin and had religious, academic, and commercial elements in its history. Eliot's grandfather, the Reverend William Greenleaf Eliot, a prominent Unitarian, had founded Washington University and became its Chancellor in 1872. Two uncles of the poet entered the ministry; his father, however, after graduating from Washington University, became a business man, although he remained responsive to the arts and given to academic charity. Washington University benefited much from his gifts. The poet's mother was herself a minor author, who published a life of her father-in-law and a poem on Savanorola and was constantly preoccupied with her literary ambitions.

The family, then, had a long history of religious and academic involvement, together with some concern for social good works. Thus Eliot was brought up among the

> . . . *symbols of Religion, the Community and Education: and I think it is a very good beginning for any child, to be brought up to reverence such institutions, and to be taught that personal and selfish aims should be subordinated to the general good which they represent.*[1]

The mother, too, was ambitious for her youngest son, whom she recognized early as having considerable talents. St. Louis, in the last years of the nineteenth century and the early years of the twentieth century, offered cultural possibilities in its mixture of New England and German elements devoted to amateur enthusiasms in the arts and philosophy. Eliot himself

[1] 'American Literature and the American Language', in *To Criticize the Critic* (London: Faber & Faber, 1965), p. 44.

received his formal education as a boy in the preparatory department of Washington University called Smith Academy:

> *It was a good school. There one was taught, as is now increasingly rare everywhere, what I consider the essentials: Latin and Greek, together with Greek and Roman history, English and American history, elementary mathematics, French and German. Also English! I am happy to remember that in those days English composition was still called* Rhetoric. *Lest you infer that the curriculum was incredibly primitive, I will add that there was a laboratory, in which physical and chemical experiments were performed successfully by the more adroit. As I failed to pass my entrance examination in physics, you will not be surprised that I have forgotten the name of the master who taught it. . . . Well! so far as I am educated, I must pay my first tribute to Smith Academy; if I had not been well taught there, I should have been unable to profit elsewhere. And so far as I am badly educated, that is attributable to laziness and caprice.*[1]

Unlike his father, uncles, brother, and several of his cousins, Eliot did not proceed to Washington University, but to Harvard. His debt to Harvard was considerable, as Mr. Herbert Howarth, in his *Notes on Some Figures Behind T. S. Eliot*,[2] has spelled out at some length. He continued with his Greek and Latin studies, studied Dante under Lowell and medieval history under Haskins, pursued an interest in French and German, and followed a course in English literature. It was at Harvard that he began to write verse and made his first acquaintanceship with the symbolist poets through reading Arthur Symons's book on the subject. Here too he participated in the 'art of local iconoclasm' which was then charac-

[1] Ibid., p. 45.
[2] A good deal of the information in the Introduction is culled from Mr. Howarth's useful book, *Notes on Some Figures Behind T. S. Eliot*.

Introduction

teristic of undergraduate society and which later bore fruit in his satiric verse on contemporary characters (such as *Portrait of a Lady*) and in his ability in poetry to draw on a range of contemporary references to the light entertainment of the day.

It was at Harvard, too, that he developed a distaste for romantic enthusiasm and the romantic temperament which enabled him to refer to himself, in mature life, as a classicist. He had already, almost instinctively, come to prefer the world of Virgil to the world of Homer on the grounds, as he revealed many years later, that 'it was a more civilised world of dignity, reason and order'. 'Dignity, reason and order' seemed increasingly remote in the developing American scene; and Eliot was temperamentally attracted to the strictures which Irving Babbitt, whose lectures he attended, laid on the 'quantitative life' to which America was being increasingly committed. Babbitt deplored the way in which the American college was adopting the habits of industry and concentrating on size, whereas 'it should impose discipline and restore reason and taste'. Nor was Eliot attracted by the democracy of elective courses; he came to consider that young men were best educated when they followed, not their interests, but disciplines imposed by more experienced minds than their own.

Clearly, then, the seeds that were later to blossom into outspoken criticisms of some of the most widely held educational beliefs of our times were sown at Harvard and may be said to have been tested in the actual experience of gaining an education. Hence, perhaps especially under the influence of Babbitt, he developed his concern for quality, his reliance on discipline and order, his distaste for eccentricity, his appreciation of the role of tradition as a means to any really secure hold on the present. The year 1910–11 he spent in France, and returned in September of the latter year to prepare for his doctorate at Harvard. In France it is likely that his reaction against the extremes of romanticism, his incipient neo-classicism, was reinforced by an awareness of the writings of men such as Charles Maurras and Julien Benda. Back at Harvard Eliot began to acquaint himself with the philosophies and literature of the East, especially those of India. He was introduced to the work of F. H. Bradley, on whom he later wrote a doctoral thesis, and his developing interest in philosophy led to an appointment as Assistant in Philosophy for the academic years 1912–13 and 1913–14. In 1914 he decided to study for a time in Germany, a project which met with the approval of the philosophy department at Harvard by whom he was now being regarded as a potential luminary; but his stay in Marburg was cut short by the war, and he proceeded to Oxford where he continued his philosophical studies and completed his thesis on Bradley.[1] Nevertheless, his interests were now gradually becoming increasingly literary once more, and although he always valued the philosophical training he had received, he now neglected its study for the writing of poetry. No doubt, however, his work in philosophy contributed to that 'reputation for affecting pedantic precision, a reputation I should not like to lose'.[2]

I have given a fairly detailed account of Eliot's upbringing and formal education because it is interesting to realize the extent to which he was formed by his mentors. Clearly, he owed them a great deal, and was mindful of the fact. He was appreciative of his school and paid specific tribute to some of his teachers at the university—such as Babbitt—by acknowledging their effect on him. In so far as education was concerned with passing on a heritage—and that is largely what the formal education of his day did comprise—he both assimi-

---

[1] The thesis was never presented for a Doctorate. It was, however, published many years later, in 1964.
[2] 'American Literature and the American Language', op. cit., p. 49.

lated and was aware of having done so. It is hard to avoid the conclusion that in the formation of the great poet, formal education played a prominent, if not a dominant, part. He was, of course, in some respects, that sort of poet; and part of the experience of his poetry is that of a man who is *living* his heritage. Quotation from others formed an essential element in the experience he was trying to convey, to summon up part of the felt experience of what it was to have been born in a particular culture, to have developed a specific memory which was part of the heightened consciousness of the twentieth century.

The rest of Eliot's life is much more common knowledge. He was married twice, suffering the tragedy of a first wife gradually sinking into madness and needing to live under restraint until her death in 1948. His second marriage was outstandingly happy and lasted until his death in 1965. He became a bank clerk in 1917 and worked in this capacity for a time. Later he became associated with the London publishing firm of Faber and Gwyer (afterwards Faber and Faber), where he was appointed a director and worked until his death. Eliot became a British citizen, but visited the United States regularly, apart from the war years. He was converted to Anglo-Catholicism, an unfashionable transformation for an eminent literary figure. Nevertheless, he did become one of the two or three outstanding literary figures of the English-speaking world and published poems, literary criticism, and works of social and educational comment. My concern with the last-named element of his work makes it of special interest that, in addition to his assistantship in philosophy at Harvard when he took 'weekly tutorial groups', he also makes it clear that he did actually for a time teach children:

> . . . *the literary dabbler has sometimes dabbled in teaching as well.*

Fundamental Issues of Education

I have been a schoolmaster, at a grammar school for one term, and for a year at a school for little boys; for three years of my life I conducted an Adult Education class once a week . . . and at a much later age I was responsible for a course for undergraduates in the subject—God forgive me—of Contemporary English Literature.[1]

It is clear that he did not find teaching altogether palatable:

I have never worked in a coal mine, or a uranium mine, or in a herring trawler; but I know from experience that working in a bank from 9:15 to 5:50, and once in four weeks the whole of Saturday, with two weeks' holiday a year, was a rest cure compared to teaching in a school.[2]

FUNDAMENTAL ISSUES OF EDUCATION

Eliot lived at a time, indeed, when the educational system was regarded as a means to the realization of a wide variety of social ideals, and when writing on education was marked by the nonchalance with which large claims were made for its effectiveness in the attainment of no doubt highly desirable but perhaps ill-defined aims. The imposition of universal schooling on the total population had been accomplished in England toward the latter part of the nineteenth century—to be precise, in the decade 1870–80. It had sprung out of a mixture of idealism and calculation—idealism concerned with the ultimate possibilities of rationality among men, once they had achieved the literacy necessary to lead them to ideas based on reason, and calculation arising out of the growing technical and bureaucratic needs of the developing industrial society. As might have been expected, calculation prevailed,

[1] 'The Aims of Education,' in *To Criticize the Critic* (London: Faber & Faber, 1965), p. 62.
[2] Ibid., p. 101.

especially in the desire to deliver the goods at the least possible cost. The resulting stir of activity in the minds of the new compulsory denizens of the schools was insufficient to produce in many much more than the barest literacy and the maximum boredom. The social conscience of the age was gradually awakened and stirred by the spectacle of underprivilege; it was not so much the education which was provided that was at fault, but the unequal terms in which it was being supplied. Hence the call for secondary schooling for all, and the 1944 Act imposing it. The movement toward 'parity of esteem' for all forms of secondary schooling was well under way, leading to those confusions of thought which the emphasis on equality of schooling for all at the age of eleven produced. If real equality was to be produced, did not this mean not only equality of provision, but also some equalization of goals? Was not the common core curriculum the essential concomitant of any equalization of means? Must not all be brought to a common experience of thought and consciousness rather than left to achieve community of outlook on the basis of half unconscious participation?

The problems of twentieth-century education in the developing technological age were not expressed in this way, of course. Nevertheless, this is what they amounted to in the total life of the nation. The basic problems were those of consciousness and rationality, and of morality and authority. The former was related to confusions about the nature of the intellectual experience the schools were to give, the latter to the way in which this experience was to be provided, and its implications for character and behaviour. Speculation on both content and procedure was rife. To what extent were children to arbitrate in their own destinies, choose their occupations, learn only through doing and involvement, not by coercion because it was 'good' for them? And in so far as education necessitates a degree of moral choice, to what extent was it to be inculcated by precept and example? To put it in the jargon of the times, was education to be subject- or child-centred? Very different *moral* as well as intellectual attitudes were implied by the distinction between the two.

If these problems of content and procedure were characteristic of the classroom, the whole nature of the relationship between education and society was implied in the developing *system* of education. The setting up of a system of education had been the first great act of state collectivism; it was to develop increasingly into an instrument of state policy. The pressures, in the West at least, were economic rather than directly political; nevertheless, in being economic they became inevitably partly political. So the relative claims of the individual and society were raised by implication. The life of the family, for instance, had already suffered diminution; education was no longer to be domestic but institutional. Increasingly the family was regarded not as the primary force in the cultural life of the next generation, but as a help or a hindrance in the business of uprooting the young from its influence. Even what and how much were to be learned were, to some degree, dependent on the 'needs' of the state. If more scientists were required for the implementation of state policies, it was the business of the educational system to provide them. Education had become an *investment*, and the state looked forward to collecting the dividends. Education was to be planned; increasingly the central government set forth the blueprints.

These are some of the fundamental issues which, overtly or covertly, have exercised educationists in our times. They form the background against which Eliot's educational theorizing took place. Characteristically, he appreciated them all, though he does not refer to them as baldly and as overtly as I have done here. He possessed the rare capacity to penetrate the surface of controversy to the underlying issues, partly because he was not only a well-read and informed member of his generation, but because he had also the peculiar insights which belonged to his chosen role as literary figure and poet.

1
The Poet

THE STRUGGLE TO COMMUNICATE

A poet is always to some degree an entertainer; but traditionally he has also been something of a seer. This latter element becomes especially prominent at the beginning of the romantic era—witness Shelly's comment on 'the unacknowledged legislator of mankind'—and it is commonly accepted today that the aim of the poet is something more important than that of mere distraction. He stands, indeed, at a peculiar focal point in the consciousness of the age in which he writes. He is concerned, first of all, with consciousness, with making people aware of things they might otherwise miss, and this through a particular medium. He is involved, that is, in the definition of certain types or categories of human experience in words.

Now language is a social phenomenon; meaning accrues to words as a result of prolonged social usage during which the scope of a particular word becomes apparent. For long periods this phenomenon is accepted quite unself-consciously by writers and others. But it is a matter that may always be about to become explicit; part of one's awareness of oneself as a social being is the need to use language for communication. The Elizabethans were very interested in the language they used, as Shakespeare bears witness (he had a great deal to say, at certain times in his career, on the significance of words), and the same has happened to us in our own times. And Eliot was one of those who draws our attention to the significance of the medium in which he wrote:

> So here I am, in the middle way, having had twenty years—
> Twenty years largely wasted, the years of *l'entre deux guerres*—
> Trying to learn to use words, and every attempt
> Is a wholly new start, and a different kind of failure
> Because one has only learnt to get the better of words
> For the thing one no longer has to say, or the way in which
> One is no longer disposed to say it.[1]

This 'intolerable wrestle with words and meanings', as he calls it elsewhere in the same poem, is merely the beginning of an awareness of other manifestations of his society which it is, in fact, the aim of his poetry to define. I would stress particularly the historical implications of the quotation on language ('. . . one has only learnt to get the better of words/*For the thing one no longer has to say*'). Eliot is concerned with ongrowth, with the uniqueness and novelty of experience and, as a result, he has to face the difficulty of defining the new in an historical coinage. Eliot was a poet intensely aware of the passage of time; he worked ultimately in an anthropological time dimension drawing, in his poetry for instance, on material gleaned by Sir J. G. Frazer in his *Golden Bough*. (In this awareness of time Eliot again resembles the Elizabethans.) And more than simply time was involved.

The two features of his work I have alluded to—his self-consciousness about language and about time—were merely symptomatic of a more general consciousness about himself and the society he inhabited, and about his relationship to that society. In other words, Eliot is typical of the poets of his day in being particularly observant of his society and of a wide

---

[1] 'East Coker' from *Four Quartets*.

variety of social manifestations. It would perhaps be even more accurate to say that he himself did a great deal to define what were to be the special preoccupations of his followers. It is true there is a sense in which he is peculiarly the poet of a certain sort of private individual experience; his Christianity, for instance, was felt with an intensity unusual in his day. But the very nature of that private experience was gradually defined in his work out of his awareness of living at a particular moment of history in a particular set of social stresses and strains. And in this he is doing nothing foreign to the practice of many poets and writers throughout the history of poetry.

A poet, then, is a man striving to define certain sorts of experience (both social and personal, and personal because social) through the exercise of a specific craft, the use of words. It is necessary to insist on the element of craft because it is partly through the exercise of craft that a man is afforded an opportunity to be on close and intimate terms with certain categories of experience which may well have a beneficial effect on his general grasp of personal and social realities. Joseph Conrad, for instance, was intimately aware that he had, in writing his novels, carried over his '. . . artistic creed from the decks of ships to the more circumscribed space of [his] desk.'[1] He had, as the world well knows, been a sea captain. When he turned writer he realized that the world of the ship and that of the desk shared a common precision:

> . . . *the man who watches the growth of the cable—a sailor's phrase which has all the force, precision, and imagery of technical language that, created by simple men with keen eyes for the real aspects of the things they see in their trade, achieves the just expression seizing upon the essential, which is the ambition of the artist in words.*[2]

[1] Joseph Conrad, 'A Familiar Preface' in *A Personal Record*.
[2] Joseph Conrad, *The Mirror of the Sea*.

The Poet

The quotation reveals precisely the sort of benefit which Eliot, like any poet, undoubtedly gathered from his own struggles with the intractable nature of his tools. To have thus to struggle, and to have triumphed so completely as Eliot has with any aspect of the common world, whether the peculiarities and idiosyncrasies of sailing ships or of words, is to receive an induction into certain *realities* of the world. A craftsman is forced to discipline himself in at least one area of his experience: much of his life is lived in contact with certain stubborn and irreducible facts of experience provided by the nature of his trade. Eliot's trade was language; his struggle might not guarantee the authenticity of his wider social understanding but it afforded some presumptive evidence of fitness to proceed.

DEFINING REALITY

A poet must not only struggle with expression; he must also have something to express. The two things go together, of course, but they are divided for the sake of analysis. Like most poets of stature, what Eliot had to express was experience of a considerable breadth and diversity. Many poets have expressed small private agonies in a memorable manner. But a great poet, to be great, needs range as well as depth, and his work is required to take on a certain representative quality. This range Eliot has. He defines important features of the modern consciousness; he defines vital characteristics of modern feelings. And he does it in a way which is itself supremely representative of his era—in Eliot the medium *and* the message are both equally representative. In referring to the medium, of course, I refer to the techniques of presentation he employs. His method of juxtaposing odd experiential fragments in such a way that they assume a representative, even symbolic, value makes him a characteristic figure. In doing so, he abandons the more usual logic of narrative, characteristic of earlier poetry. Here is the modern 'all-at-once-ness' long before Marshall McLuhan was ever heard of—past, present, and future, near and far, present and absent, all jostle in adjacent lines to form that picture of the modern world which the next forty years was to spend its time tediously spelling out, almost unconscious that it had all been represented in a poem published in 1922.

The poem I refer to is, of course, *The Waste Land*, which defined our modern disillusionment—or our illusion, as Eliot put it with his usual subtlety, of being disillusioned. Here is the forerunner of all of our recent awareness of existential absurdity; here is the joyless sex, the vapidity of a 'good-time' civilization, the protest and the emptiness as it has come overtly to pass since Eliot wrote. Here is the kaleidoscopic presentation of different cultural levels, of sexual ambiguity, of merging and mingling which democratic formlessness has fostered long before most people were even aware of such features of our common life. Today they are commonplace, but Eliot long before created in images thrown together in skilful juxtapositions the very *feel* of such a society. And it is this capacity to define feelings relevant to the particular stage of the development of a society that, as Eliot himself points out in his essay on 'The Social Function of Poetry', the true power of the poet to educate is manifest.

An illustration will serve to ward off, at the beginning of this book, any impression that a poet is necessarily a wild-eyed long-haired creature, essentially remote and abstracted from his times. This is a romantic view of the poet—and it was rarely true even of the romantics. It certainly was not true of Eliot, who was, as I have indicated, anti-romantic in many of his attitudes and always stressed his classicism. (Not the least of Mr. Eliot's contributions to literature, his friend Ronald Duncan said, was the cleanliness of his collars.) And when we look more closely at his technique of presentation, we find it curiously reminiscent of the first great new cultural form of the twentieth century, the cinema. Ezra Pound defines for us how this novel form of the cinema expressed something characteristic of modern life, in a comment on Cocteau's *Poésies*:

> *The life of a village is narrative, you have not been there three weeks before you know that in the revolution et cetera, and when M. le Comte et cetera, and so forth. In a city the visual impressions succeed each other, overlap, overcross, they are 'cinematographic'.*[1]

It is interesting to remember that it was Ezra Pound who was responsible for the final 'cutting' of Eliot's original version of his poem. On Pound's advice he shortened it considerably, and thus enhanced its cinematographic quality.

Here are the first eighteen lines from *The Waste Land* which will indicate what I mean:

> April is the cruellest month, breeding
> Lilacs out of the dead land, mixing
> Memory and desire, stirring
> Dull roots with spring rain.
> Winter kept us warm, covering
> Earth in forgetful snow, feeding
> A little life with dried tubers.
> Summer surprised us, coming over the Starnbergersee
> With a shower of rain; we stopped in the colonnade,
> And went on in sunlight, into the Hofgarten,
> And drank coffee, and talked for an hour.
> Bin gar keine Russin, stamm' aus Litauen, echt deutsch.
> And when we were children, staying at the archduke's,

[1] Quoted by H. Howarth, *Notes on Some Figures Behind T. S. Eliot*, p. 236.

Defining Reality

My cousin's, he took me out on a sled,
And I was frightened. He said, Marie,
Marie, hold on tight. And down we went.
In the mountains, there you feel free.
I read, much of the night, and go south in the winter.[1]

The poem starts with a generalization which nevertheless has
the force of an immediate experience; April *is* 'the cruellest
month'—this is also a personal and a particular experience,
because it is directly contemporary. 'The snows of winter kept
us warm' refers to the recent past; it is part of the same feeling
of significance, applicable by contrast to present discontent.
Here is the writer's consciousness in the here and now reflect-
ing on his immediate circumstances, so that he not only
remembers and desires but is aware of doing so. It is not any
particular reminiscence or any specific wish that distresses,
but merely the unease of remembering and wanting things.
But then an actual memory intervenes and in a flashback we
are in some previous summer, in carefree conversation, over-
hearing the chatter of our neighbours. Then a further flashback to the childhood, to a frightening experience in the
mountains on a sled. 'Down we went' has the multi-dimen-
sional significance that double or triple superimposed images
on the screen have. We went down the mountain; we traversed
rapidly the layers of memory to juxtapose and link past thrills
and present discontent; all Europe went 'down the drain' in
the recent war—this last meaning in the background but dis-
cernible. This reminiscence of mountains contrasts former
freedom with present constrictions: the inability to sleep and
the conventional health-seeking tour of the winter. In each
case the transition is immediate, unexplained—one makes
one's sense as one does of contrasting images on a cinema

[1] *The Waste Land*, ll. 1–18.

screen; and the logic is the logic of images, no longer the continuity of discourse. *The Waste Land* is full of hints for a film. M. Alain Robbe-Grillet defined some essential characteristic of this type of writing (though over forty years later) when he urged the significance of 'Posters, shop windows, anything stuck on the walls all around us. I believe these images constitute our profundity. . . . The essence of modern man is no longer to be found within a hidden soul, but plastered on hoardings. . . . Therefore, study the surface, the object, for it contains the only answer.' Eliot, of course, is profunder than this implies; his images are chosen to reverberate in the mind, to reveal an essence, they do not remain on the surface. Even M. Robbe-Grillet admits his inability to dissolve thus into his surroundings: 'One is always a little nineteenth century. I too have a soul, after all.' This comes from the part creator of one of the profoundest of modern films: *L'Année dernière à Marienbad*, a film curiously Eliotic in its exploration of loneliness and memory through images—a loneliness grown more desperate because less ironic than that implicit in another Eliot poem, *The Love Song of J. Alfred Prufrock*.

For, of course, the protagonist of *L'Année Dernière* is too desperately inside the experience for irony; whereas Prufrock knows (in his own words) he is 'not Prince Hamlet'—he is not, that is, an heroic figure, but

> . . . an attendant lord, one that will do
> To swell a progress, start a scene or two.

He sees himself, that is to say, with a certain irony, as a trifle ridiculous, 'Almost, at times, the Fool'. This is a very self-conscious person, one who is slightly pathetic and knows it.

And, indeed, it is through his capacity for irony that Eliot can assimilate the vulgarities of the world and 'place' them.

Defining Reality

It is very much the kaleidoscope of the modern world that he sees in *The Waste Land*; neurotic women in wealthy houses, worn out child-bearing working-class women in pubs, city workers on their way to their offices on winter mornings, visits to society clairvoyants, seductions in bed-sitting-rooms, scraps of ragtime. This is the waste land of modern existence in its lack of any sort of spiritual fulfilment, and the 'camera' picks out one scene after another for its representative quality and cumulative effect. But more is at work than simply a camera in words; the experiences recorded are also placed in a time dimension of human history. This waste land is not only the modern urban scene; it is also the unfruitful and infertile land of primitive races whose kings have lost their virility—as we have lost our King—and who thus, in accordance with ancient beliefs, face a parched and barren future. It is also the world of Greek mythology ('I Tiresias') and Roman history ('You who were with me in the ships at Mylae'), Elizabethan England and other 'withered stumps of time'. The partial effect is to give the poem a representative quality: this is a basic human experience, a search for meaning which is taking place, not an accident of a single moment of time. But often the historical echoes exercise a controllingly ironic effect, for they imply to us how we are to understand the scene. At the beginning of the passage describing the rich neurotic woman there is evoked a brief reminiscence of a previous glittering figure:

> The Chair she sat in, like a burnished throne
> Glowed on the marble . . .

This reminds us of Shakespeare's Cleopatra:

> The barge she sat in, like a burnished throne
> Burnt on the water . . .

31

The contrast emphasizes the hard artificial quality of the modern scene when we contrast Eliot's heavily ornate description with Shakespeare's limpid flowing lines; Eliot's woman is tortured and unsure, bored and restless, Cleopatra supremely confident and radiant; the very air itself had gone to gaze on her. But the modern woman seeks the sanctity of the 'closed car at ten'.

History and historical allusion is used, then, not only to stress the continuity of problems relevant to the human condition, but also to contrast more vital and heady ages with our present discontents. We are shown to be undergoing a profound spiritual malaise which mankind encounters from time to time; we also see this in a perspective which hints at alternative possibilities. We see present discontent as a recognizable phase of the human cycle, but we do not see it as an inevitable concomitant of the human condition. At the very least, the mind of the poet is larger than the sickness he diagnoses.

THE NEED TO RECOGNIZE TRADITION

But it is a sickness—and this perhaps comes as a shock to those of us who have been nurtured on ideas of perpetual progress. Admittedly, Eliot was writing at the end of a long and terrible war—the greatest and the bloodiest in history; in a sense he represents the exhaustion of a particular moment of time. But he also points to something more fundamental which goes beyond a temporary sense of desolation. It is striking that he never refers directly to the war itself, for what he attempts to diagnose is something even deeper than the experience of war, something of which the war is perhaps itself a portent. He is diagnosing the modern soul and the modern experience, its kaleidoscopic impressionism, its lack of any real roots, its essential incoherence. It is as if he is asserting that the only formative agent in the midst of all this incoherence is his own mind, a mind nurtured on a historical time scale which sees hope only in the complexity of the past, assured by past vitalities which surely, by implication, can come again. But for the present there is only stoicism and endurance: 'Give, sympathise, control.'

Now it would be a very superficial view to dismiss this as the perverted hysteria of a single man: too many others since Eliot wrote have borne out his picture. There have been further wars, political upheavals, spiritual sicknesses like drug taking, a wild and hysterical pop scene of trivial and superficial distraction ('O O O O that Shakespeherian Rag'); even the journalists have long grown accustomed to referring to the 'crisis of our times'. Nor did Eliot himself simply present the sickness; even in *The Waste Land* he begins to move toward a positive affirmation, as I have just very briefly shown. Certainly here it is very little more than a gesture; in general what exists as positive is little other than a nostalgia for more vital times. But as he developed as a poet, so his work increased in complexity, he was more fully able to hold the sickness in balance and to reaffirm more positive possibilities which his own spiritual pilgrimage revealed. Though there was much that was personal in this, there was also a reawakening of roots; memory led to a renewal of a certain desire which he did not always regret.

What in fact took place was development, not a radical reorientation; the author of the *Four Quartets* is demonstrably the writer of *The Waste Land*; his later poems almost constitute a mediation on the earlier. He come to accept the disparity of experience, its fragmentary quality, its mingling of 'memory and desire' or, to put it another way, of history and affirmation. He sees, indeed, that *this is the human condition:* always to be involved in a state of tension between the various dimensions of the human consciousness—a consciousness that looks forward yet paradoxically only does so in terms learned from the past, that seeks affirmation but is inevitably involved in the pull toward negation and evil, that changes and yet exists within a core of the changeless.

In a 'Commentary' which he contributed to his magazine, *The Criterion*, for October 1932, Eliot reflects on a dictum culled from a book by Curtius: 'The Permanent Has Come to Mean Paralysis and Death.' The awareness of conflict between change and permanence is, he says, a very old one, going back to pre-Socratic days; but far from seeing in change a value in itself, Eliot considers that one of our main tasks is to work out 'the delicate relation of the Eternal and the Transient'. The following, on the subject of art, indicates why the past mattered so much to him—for what it had brought forth in art and conduct could never be surpassed; it could only be redefined in equal though different terms. We must know:

> *That there can be no art greater than the art which has already been created: there will only be different and necessarily different combinations of the eternal and the changing in the forms of art. That men individually can never attain anything higher than has already been attained among the Saints; but that in any place, in any time, another Saint may be born. Such a just perception of the permanent relations of the Enduring and the Changing should on the one hand make us realise our own time in better proportion to times past and times to come: we are now inclined to think of our own age and moment as hysterically as people did in the year 1000. And on the other hand it should help us to think better of our own time, as not isolated or unique, and remind us that fundamentally our individual problems and duties are the same as they have been for others at any time—and equally our opportunities.*[1]

[1] Howarth, op. cit., pp. 269–70.

The Need to Recognize Tradition

One takes his point. In science we progress, so that change is not simply alteration but development—Einstein goes beyond Newton. But no one will ever replace Shakespeare or in any way supersede him; even the cave paintings of Lascaux are not preliminary sketches for a more sophisticated, 'truer' model in later ages; as they stand they are irreplaceable. It is little wonder that Eliot failed to think of change exclusively as progress.

Yet also, paradoxically, he realized the need for change. In a society oriented toward the new he re-emphasized the need for tradition; equally he asserted quite categorically that 'Tradition cannot mean standing still'. He speaks in one of his poems of the 'still point of a turning world', thus symbolizing that sense of eternity even in time, of the static even in the midst of movement, which indicated among other things how he saw life so often in terms of a tension of opposites. This, largely, was to be the theme of his last great group of poems, *The Four Quartets*. We need continually to face new situations, tackle new problems; but we can only do so in terms of the wisdom which we have acquired from the past. Into the future, then, the present and the past are inevitably projected; nothing is entirely new, but nothing is entirely renewed—this is the paradox in terms of which we live:

> Time present and time past
> Are both perhaps present in time future,
> And time future contained in time past.[1]

Eliot's central assumption in these last poems is that contained in the Christian world view. By 1928, he had become an Anglo-Catholic in religion as well as a royalist in politics and a classicist in literature. Christianity is a religion which

---

[1] 'Burnt Norton' from *Four Quartets*, ll. 1–3.

sees life in terms of struggle symbolized by the archetypal conflict between man's original state of sin and the possibilities of grace. As a dweller in both the natural and the transcendental world man finds no consolation in the idea of human perfectibility and hence not in any notion of the inevitability of progress. Human actions can, of course, be for better and for worse; but even at best they are inevitably tainted by self-regard, like his own Beckett in *Murder in the Cathedral*, who puts aside temptation, although in the very act of doing so he sees the corruption implicit in the martyrdom offered him by his rejection; even our highest actions are tainted by self-esteem.

It is not surprising, then, that he saw life in terms of the antinomies which revealed the paradoxical nature of human thought and behaviour. His sense of the assimilation yet incompatibility of opposites lies at the heart of the poetic experience of these four great poems:

> . . . Only by the form, the pattern,
> Can words or music reach
> The stillness, as a Chinese vase still
> Moves perpetually in its stillness.
> Not the stillness of the violin, while the note lasts,
> Not that only, but the co-existence,
> Or say that the end precedes the beginning,
> And the end and the beginning were always there
> Before the beginning and after the end,
> And all is always now.[1]

The Quartets are full of opposed concepts: words like 'from' and 'towards', 'movement' and 'arrest', 'past' and 'future' recur in paradoxical juxtaposition:

> Only through time time is conquered.

[1] Ibid., Section V.

The Creative Use of Struggle

THE CREATIVE USE OF STRUGGLE

For Eliot, then, man is both at home and a stranger in the world, part of both the natural and the transcendental orders. In defining man's position in these terms he differs from many social thinkers of his day who seek an ultimate reconciliation between man and the social order. The Marxists, for instance, look forward to the ultimate withering away of the state, symbol of a fundamental imbalance between man's desires and the requirements of society. The idea of man being able to live in 'uncomplicated adjustment to an uncomplicated world' is ruled out entirely by Eliot largely because man is a citizen of another kingdom with its own unique demands, as well as of the earthly one. For Eliot, seeing in man a conflict between the impulse to rigid order and the impulse to disintegration and chaos, the most favourable condition was that in which these opposing forces achieved a temporary and necessarily unstable balance, the still point, to revert to a previous allusion, in a turning world. 'The danger of freedom is deliquescence; the danger of strict order is petrifaction.'

Now, all this is fundamental to his social criticism and theorizing. I have already drawn attention, briefly, to his poetic picture of our present society; he sees in it a waste land, spiritually dessicated, its people seeking distraction. The characters who inhabit his poems are usually bored, dissatisfied, caught in a trap ('I think we are in rat's alley'); or they are timid, unsure of themselves, like Mr. Prufrock ('Do I dare to eat a peach?'); or they fulfil an empty, slightly pretentious social round like the Lady of 'Portrait of a Lady' when the 'conversation slips / Among velleities and carefully caught regrets'. Among these relaxations and decadences the Divine Mystery demands a different, sterner response:

37

The Poet

   . . . were we led all that way for
Birth or Death? There was a Birth, certainly,
We had evidence and no doubt. I had seen birth and death,
But had thought they were different; this Birth was
Hard and bitter agony for us, like Death, our death.
We returned to our places, these Kingdoms
But no longer at ease here, in the old dispensation,
With an alien people clutching their gods.
I should be glad of another death.[1]

A curious, divinely ordered unease, then, is at the heart of
Eliot's experience of life. And this makes him see, for instance,
that human creativity is not simply a matter of expression,
an outpouring of feeling, an indulgence in emotion, but a
struggle, a 'wrestle with words', a reconciliation of opposites:
disharmony is as necessary as harmony for the creative spirit.
'Fortunate the man who, at the right moment, meets the right
friend; fortunate also the man who at the right moment meets
the right enemy.'[2]

Now in his social theorizing Eliot is concerned to define the
creative society (I am tempted to say the 'educative society'),
one whose aim is not adjustment and the elimination of
struggle, but the creative use of struggle. Conflict and irritation have as important roles to play as harmony and collabora-
tion; they are, in any case, all part of the human condition.
Thus he is not an egalitarian because this would mean doing
away with the conflict between classes. This conflict, he thinks,
surprisingly in an age when equality has become one of the
prime virtues, has formative and productive possibilities,
although he wants a class structure of that degree of fluidity
which will at once preserve social continuity without de-

[1] From 'The Journey of the Magi'.
[2] *Notes Towards the Definition of Culture* (London: Faber & Faber, 1948),
p. 59.

generating into the petrifaction of a caste system on the one hand or the delinquescence of excessive social mobility on the other. In the same way he wishes that nationalism be tempered by regionalism to encourage just the right amount of provincial independence without disintegration into a number of local cultures. Again, churchman though he is, he wants a 'church capable of conflict with the state as well as co-operation with it'. And so he comes to a theory of the importance of friction in his revitalized society:

At this point I introduce a new notion: that of the vital importance for a society of friction between its parts. Accustomed as we are to think in figures of speech taken from machinery, we assume that a society, like a machine, should be as well-oiled as possible, provided with ball bearings of the best steel. We think of friction as waste of energy. I shall not attempt to substitute any other imagery: perhaps at this point the less we think in analogies the better. In the last chapter I suggested that in any society which became permanently established in either a caste or a classless system, the culture would decay: one might even put it that a classless society should always be emerging into class, and a class society should be tending towards obliteration of its class distinctions. I now suggest that both class and region, by dividing the inhabitants of a country into two different kinds of groups, lead to a conflict favourable to creativeness and progress. And (to remind the reader of what I said in my introduction) these are only two of an indefinite number of conflicts and jealousies which should be profitable to society. Indeed, the more the better: so that everyone should be an ally of everyone else in some respects, and an opponent in several others, and no one conflict, envy or fear will dominate.[1]

He concludes with a characteristic paradox: 'The universality of irritation is the best assurance of peace.' Nor is it only

[1] Ibid., pp. 58–9.

within the various geographical, social, and institutional aspects of society the there is need of this creative disharmony; a similar tension has a fruitful role to play within the mind of the individual. Even within the totality of the Christian Society, in Christendom itself, the unity which exists should allow for some diversity and even some conflict in theology; 'for it is only by the struggle against constantly appearing false ideas that the truth is enlarged and clarified, and in the conflict with heresy that orthodoxy is developed to meet the needs of the time'.[1]

This brief allusion to his views on the functioning of society, amplified in the next chapter, is necessary to show the part played by the concrete experience of the creative writer. His social views—one is constantly brought up against this fact—are not abstractions derived from some socio-political theory remote from the pressures of actual living, but spring out of a personal creative effort and a mind sufficiently conscious of itself to reflect on the general implications of its own particular experience. That is why some understanding of the nature of his poetry, however brief, is essential to an understanding of his social views; and an understanding of his social views are fundamental to an appreciation of his educational ones. Clearly there is usually a close connection between educational and social theories, for education as we realize it through our system of schooling is a social phenomenon; it is sustained by the state and established to meet the 'needs' of society and to enable young people to take their places in a social order. John Dewey is a supreme example of an educationist whose views are directed to making the school an instrument for the implementation (and even the initiation) of social, democratic policies and behaviour. What to my mind makes Eliot an infinitely more rewarding writer both on society and on educa-

[1] Ibid., p. 82.

tion lies in his superior grasp of the nature of the human situation; and this precisely because he was the sort of poet I have tried to describe here, with not only an intense awareness of the perennial paradox of the human predicament but with an ability to grasp with incredible intuitive sureness, and to define the peculiar forms in which the human dilemma has revealed itself in this century through his medium of language. The 'progressive' writers on education have always been right to stress the relationship between education and life. However, they have gone astray in their inability to catch convincingly the feel of living either in general terms, or at a particular moment of history. Important though Rousseau is as an educational theorist, his *Emile* reveals little understanding of human relationships or even, oddly enough, of children. The child Emile is a pure abstraction, idealized to conform to Rousseau's own projected plan of upbringing. Though he realized and emphasized some aspects of child nature in the abstract—its love of activity, its capacity for curiosity, for example—he never gives us the feel of what it is like to be a child; and his view of the developing Emile involves passages of appalling sentimentality which were falsified in experience, as Richard Edgeworth and others discovered when they tried to put Rousseau's precepts into practice. In the same way, Dewey's understanding of the industrial-bureaucratic state, which is the society for which he is preparing his young people, is deficient in subtlety. He does not fully appreciate the nature and impact of industry but falls back on sentimentalities drawn from pre-industrial modes of organization. In a sense he never altogether freed himself from the idealized picture of the log cabin, and too often thought that the involvement in domestic and social activities characteristic of those days was still viable in the changed social and economic conditions of industrialization. He failed also to accept the tensions implicit

2
Eliot's Social Views

THE HISTORICAL SENSE: CULTURAL CONTINUITY

In the first chapter I was inevitably led from a consideration of Eliot's poetry to a preliminary incursion into his views on the social and political problems of his times, for his personal agony is not to be thought of simply as a private experience but as socially relevant to the dilemmas of his day and age. Out of the tension of opposites which characterized his inner experience arose a realization of the universal applicability of both disharmony and reconciliation as perennial factors in man's social strivings. Society, indeed, can only be meaningfully and fruitfully understood by those who start from a proper appreciation of the individual human dilemma, not by those who ignore the paradoxes of life in favour of some abstract and unrealistic belief in the possibility of total harmony and adjustment. Man is born to live in unease, and that unease is bound to be reflected in any fruitful thinking about human problems. Eliot believed, of course, that society could be organized on better or worse lines; but the theme that haunts him is that even at best the life of the world will only be a travesty of what can be imagined. The statement of the ideal must therefore always be tempered by the apprehension of the actual. It is true that in his prose writings he was perhaps more conscious of the need to examine the possibilities of the ideal, '. . . whereas in the writing of verse one can only deal with actuality'. But it is in a sense the very disenchantment

43

which runs as an undertone through Eliot's exposition of his ideal, the constant reminders of the empirical actual, which accounts for the coolness of tone and of his exposition, the scepticism which breaks through now and again as an uncertainty of intent ('If and perhaps and but'), and identifies the hand of the poet in the prose of the idealist. And this means that the ideal itself appears as a victory plucked from the sordidness of the actual, not a glib formulation of impossible desiderata. Eliot has none of the self-deceiving word spinning of the typical utopian, but a tempered and measured *gravitas* which controls his flights into the realm of the desirable. His sense of history is too strong. Even if we find some of his ideas so against the trends of current social fashion as to appear unrealistic, we have to admit that they do not transcend possibilities of human organization; indeed, these possibilities have been demonstrated within a comparatively recent time scale, and we are left with the uneasy feeling that it is perhaps we who are eccentric, not he.

These traits can be illustrated by a fuller consideration of his concept of tradition and his reaction against liberalism. It is entirely typical that his attack on liberalism, fundamental though it is to his whole way of thinking, should nevertheless contain an element of equivocation, of ambiguity. Liberalism he finds to be the characteristic creed of modern Western society, where the social order is defined very much in terms of what it is *against* rather than what it is *for*; a lack of positive beliefs is a prime feature of our age. We inhabit a 'negative' society, and this negativity is something which derives from liberalism:

> *which tends to release energy rather than accumulate it, to relax rather than to fortify. It is a movement not so much defined by its end, as by its starting point; away from, rather than towards, some-*

thing definite. Our point of departure is more real to us than our destination.[1]

Its worst fault lies in the nature of the vacuum it creates:

> *By destroying traditional social habits of the people, by dissolving their natural collective consciousness into individual constituents, by licensing the opinions of the most foolish, by substituting instruction for education, by encouraging cleverness rather than wisdom, the upstart rather than the qualified, by fostering a notion of getting on to which the alternative is hopeless apathy, Liberalism can prepare the way for that which is its own negation: the artificial, mechanised or brutalised control which is a desperate remedy for its chaos.*[2]

Eliot's point is that some sort of control is essential—man needs both freedom and order, and the quality of the freedom will be intimately bound up with the quality of the order he accepts. He sees, in fact, that the notion of freedom is ambiguous—it involves 'freedom to' as well as 'freedom from'; any free qualitative response to the conditions of human existence presupposes the initial restraints which alone make possible the concern for worth and value.

But he also sees that liberalism is not a stance simply to be abandoned—it does in fact have a negative role to perform. It prevents, for instance, the imposition of the wrong sort of order in that it creates the conditions under which men can freeely choose the order best suited to them. Hence the answer to liberalism is not simply conservatism; for if liberalism by itself implies chaos, conservatism can mean petrifaction. How, then, can we resolve this polarity? Eliot's answer lies in an appeal to tradition; and as the notion of tradition is one which plays a very fundamental part in his social thinking, it will be

---

[1] *The Idea of a Christian Society* (London: Faber & Faber, 1939), p. 15.
[2] Ibid., p. 16.

necessary to augment considerably the brief allusions made in the last chapter.

His problem is that the tendency of unlimited industrialism is

> ... *to create bodies of men and women—of all classes—detached from tradition, alienated from religion, and susceptible to mass suggestion: in other words a mob. And a mob will be no less a mob if it is well fed, well clothed, well housed, and well disciplined.*[1]

Generalizing about his own experience as a poet, he had already, in his literary essays, shown the importance of an understanding of tradition and of working within an inherited framework, if a writer were to produce anything of permanent value. What this means he defines in his famous essay, 'Tradition and the Individual Talent':

> *Tradition ... cannot be inherited, and if you want it you must obtain it by great labour. It involves, in the first place, the historical sense, which we may call nearly indispensable to anyone who would continue to be a poet beyond his twenty-fifth year; and the historical sense involves a perception, not only of the pastness of the past, but of its presence; the historical sense compels a man to write not merely with his own generation in his bones, but with a feeling that the whole of the literature of his own country has a simultaneous existence and composes a simultaneous order. This historical sense, which is a sense of the timeless as well as of the temporal and of the timeless and of the temporal together, is what makes a writer traditional. And it is at the same time what makes a writer most acutely conscious of his place in time, of his own contemporaneity.*[2]

Several features of this view of tradition and its role in the life of the poet are of interest. In the first place, tradition is

[1] Ibid., p. 21.
[2] Reprinted in *Selected Essays*.

clearly the product of education—it must be obtained 'by great labour'. Secondly, his use of the word is certainly normative; an understanding of tradition is a valuable, indeed, an essential, acquisition in the life of a poet. Thirdly, the historical sense constitutes a crucial element in the definition of contemporaneity, a paradox of which the young are often far too unaware. We cannot sense the meaning of our times without seeing them as participating in a continuum; and we cannot appreciate the form of the continuum without a sense of 'before' as well as of 'after'.

But tradition is not something inert with which we must simply come to terms. Nothing is more important in Eliot's view of tradition than his belief that even tradition itself is subject to change. It must, in a sense, be so because as the generations succeed one another, tradition itself must inevitably be viewed from slightly different viewpoints. Any new addition to the traditional in the form of a new work of art, by the very act of its novelty, and by the force of its intervention, involves a shift in human consciousness and enables us to see the past in a slightly different way. What goes to form the mind of the artist is derived from the inherited wisdom of the race; at the same time, such a mind is representative of more than the past. Eliot spells out the nature of the paradox:

> *He [the poet] must be aware that the mind of Europe—the mind of his own country—a mind which he learns in time to be very much more important than his own private mind—is a mind which changes and that this change is a development which abandons nothing en* route, *which does not superannuate either Shakespeare, or Homer, or the rock drawing of the Magdalenian draughtsmen.*[1]

It was partly to cope with this notion of change in our appre-

[1] From 'Tradition and the Individual Talent'.

ciation of the past that Eliot, at a later stage, in *After Strange Gods*, developed the notion of orthodoxy to supplement that of tradition. It meant splitting his former view of the nature of tradition into its conscious and unconscious elements. The term is now applied to the largely unconscious factors, '. . . a way of feeling and acting which characterises a group throughout a generation.' He sees it as comprising '. . . all those habitual actions, habits and customs, from the most significant religious rites to our conventional way of greeting a stranger which represent a blood kinship of "the same people living in the same place".' We become conscious of tradition only when its manifestations are beginning to fall into disuse. Hence the danger that tradition, being so largely unconscious, may seem to be hostile to change; what we are not aware of we cannot easily alter. In fact, however, 'Tradition cannot mean standing still'; tradition truly defined is not something inert, but includes a dynamic element which enables these unconscious elements to work meaningfully in order to produce coherence in an age or a personality. To assert the importance of tradition, in fact, is '. . . to aim to stimulate the life which produced' the real and the vital in any age; it is not to take over wholesale the values of some far off and vanished era, or to indulge in a sentimental attitude towards the past:

> For one thing, in even the very best living tradition there is always a mixture of good and bad. . . . What we can do is to use our minds, remembering that a tradition without intelligence is not worth having, to discover what is the best life for us not as a political abstraction, but as a particular people in a particular place.[1]

Thus we must supplement the acceptance of tradition by the conscious critical awareness of orthodoxy:

[1] *After Strange Gods* (London: Faber & Faber, 1934), p. 19,

The Historical Sense: Cultural Continuity

*Tradition by itself is not enough; it must be perpetually criticised
and brought up to date under the supervision of what I call orthodoxy;*[1]

for the crucial feature of orthodoxy lies in the way it calls 'for
the exercise of all our conscious intelligence'. If tradition is of
the blood, orthodoxy is of the brain: 'In the co-operation of
both is the reconciliation of thought and feeling.'

Another way of putting this would be to say that the correc-
tions of orthodoxy ensure that 'tradition' remains a normative
concept. Clearly, there is a danger that 'tradition' may sustain
good and bad elements; checked by orthodoxy it will shed
what is trivial or of transient significance. Eliot's supporting
illustrations, intended to reveal the corrective power of tradition refined by orthodoxy, are drawn from literature rather
than from politics or social activities; but his literary figures
take on a representative quality, and prove in some cases
symptomatic of a malaise to which we are all prone: the infla-
tion of the personal at the expense of the wisdom of the race,
the exploitation of our individuality uncorrected by a sense of
social fitness or decorum. The writer is treated as a representative citizen of the modern world, subject to its pressures
and revelatory of its shortcomings and eccentricities. Hence
the faults of the writer have a more general implication:

*What is disastrous is that the writer should deliberately give rise to
his 'individuality', that he should even cultivate his differences from
others; and that his readers should cherish the author of genius, not
in spite of his deviations from the inherited wisdom of the race, but
because of them.*[2]

Eliot illustrates this judgment by an analysis of three stories

[1] Ibid., p. 62.
[2] Ibid., p. 33.

49

by contemporary writers—Katherine Mansfield, D. H. Lawrence, and James Joyce, who demonstrate a range of possible reactions to their times. He finds Lawrence to be '. . . an almost perfect example of a heretic,' and Joyce '. . . the most ethically orthodox of the more eminent writers of my time.' Lawrence's characters betray a lack of respect for moral obligations, are unfurnished with a conscience, in contrast to an orthodoxy of sensibility which marks Joyce's creations. Eliot generalizes his comment on his individual authors by suggesting that

> . . . *with the disappearance of the idea of original Sin, with the disappearance of the idea of intense moral struggle, the human beings represented to us both in poetry and in prose fiction today, and more patently among the serious writers than in the underworld of letters, tend to become less and less real. It is in fact in moments of moral and spiritual struggle depending upon spiritual sanctions, rather than in those 'bewildering minutes' in which we are all very much alike, that men and women come nearest to being real. If you do away with this struggle, and maintain that by tolerance, benevolence, inoffensiveness and a redistribution or increase of purchasing power, combined with a devotion, on the part of an élite, to Art, the world will be as good as anyone could require, then you must expect human beings to become more and more vaporous.*[1]

What in fact he thought writers like Lawrence suffered from was the 'crippling effect . . . of not having been brought up in the environment of a living and central tradition'. Here the notion of tradition, glossed by its two approbatory adjectives, resumes its normative functioning.

It is usual today to deprecate *After Strange Gods* as one of Eliot's less happy exercises; and indeed he later expressed some distaste for it. Nevertheless it helps to define his general

[1] Ibid., p. 42.

position in an interesting way. Whereas it was explicitly Lawrence's aim to break out of what he termed 'the fixed moral
scheme', to explore below the 'old stable ego of the character'
(as he said in defence of *The Rainbow*: 'I only care about what
the woman is—what she is—inhumanly, physiologically,
materially'), it is just as explicitly Eliot's aim to reassert the
traditional categories, to place the current personal and social
crisis within a time-scale which accepted the historical culture
and its moral (specifically Christian) imperatives. If tradition
doesn't mean standing still, it doesn't mean breaking loose,
either. Thus,

> . . . *when morals cease to be a matter of tradition and orthodoxy—
> that is, of the habits of the community formulated, corrected and
> elevated by the continuous thought and direction of the Church—
> and when each man is to elaborate his own, then* personality *becomes
> a thing of alarming importance.*[1]

His subsequent comment on Lawrence, whom Eliot considered (not altogether fairly) to have '. . . started life wholly
free from any restriction of tradition or institution' indicates
clearly his distaste for idiosyncratic personal judgment dependent upon 'the Inner Light', the '. . . most untrustworthy
and deceitful guide that ever offered itself to wandering
humanity'.

These views are of great interest at a time when ideas of
moral autonomy and individual self-expression are much
recommended in the world of education. It will have become
clear that it is a fundamental mistake to see Eliot as an ex-
ponent of a static society concerned simply to preserve out-
ward forms at the cost of inward petrifaction. The role he
assigns to orthodoxy alone, involving consciousness and critical

[1] Ibid., p. 54.

51

capacity, is proof enough of my contention. It provides evidence of his awareness of the conflicts between inherited forms and the novelty of experience—and of the need to recognize that novelty. There is even the statement in *After Strange Gods* itself, despite its emphasis on orthodoxy and tradition, that

> *... perfect orthodoxy in the individual artist is not always necessary, or even desirable. In many instances it is possible that an indulgence of eccentricities is the condition of the man's saying anything at all.*[1]

Nevertheless, one comes back to the need to revivify *within* the traditional framework, to operate within the current 'forms'. Hence the emphasis, unusual in current educational discussion, on the importance of right habits of behaviour—an emphasis which contrasts sharply with present insistence on the importance of autonomous rational decision as the basis of moral behaviour. Eliot's criticism of the contemporary interest in personality is not an eccentric foray expressing his distaste for certain authors, but part of a consistent attempt to define the role of the creative artist—and hence of the self-conscious individual—in a disintegrating society. His distaste for 'personality' is consistent with his attempt to reassert a continuity of standards necessary in the definition of a more truly vital, and therefore more educative, society than the one we presently inhabit:

> *The first requisite usually held up by the promoters of personality is that a man should 'be himself'; and this 'sincerity' is considered more important than that the self in question should, socially and spiritually, be a good or a bad one. This view of personality is merely an assumption on the part of the modern world, and is no more tenable than several other views which have been held at various*

[1] Ibid., p. 32.

times and in several places. The personality thus expressed, the personality which fascinates us in the work of philosophy or art, tends naturally to be the unregenerate *personality, partly self-deceived and partly irresponsible, and because of its freedom, terribly* limited *by prejudice and self-conceit, capable of much good or great mischief according to the natural goodness or impurity of the man: and we are all, naturally, impure. All that I have been able to do here is to suggest that there are standards of criticism, not ordinarily in use, which we may apply to whatever is offered to us as works of philosophy or of art, which might help to render them safer and more profitable for us.*[1]

He sees that the current role assigned to the artist—one of 'Olympian elevation and superior indifference ... which I can only imperfectly understand'—is symptomatic of malaise rather than peculiar to the artist's calling.

We are, in fact, brought back full circle to the social order without positive beliefs, 'worm eaten with liberalism'. The gap, it is now clear, can be partly filled by a respect for the presentness of the past. For the notion of progress and of the superseding of the past, which is clearly relevant to the development of the sciences, has no such acceptable application to the progress of the arts. The great works of the past form a permanent collection of achievements which can be added to, not superseded. History—tradition—is something positive in the life of the present, not simply something to be discarded as irrelevant and restrictive: and yet it is not the whole of the present, which must exist in its own terms as well as in those it has inherited.

A CONSERVATIVE DEFINITION OF POLITICS

These views constitute an important corrective to develop-

[1] Ibid., pp. 62–3.

mental and growth theories which, deeply influenced by nineteenth-century evolutionism arising out of Darwinian biology, have profoundly affected thinking about education. Education is an undertaking which affects individual growth, and to that extent constitutes a developing process to which the concept of 'progress' is clearly applicable. However we define the word, we clearly expect the pupil in some way or other to be 'better' as a result of his education. It is not then surprising to find such evolutionary notions applied not only to the education of an individual but also to education as a *system* of universal schooling. With the injunction to adapt the system of education to changing social conditions has often gone the presumption that such an adaptation necessarily involves an improvement. What Eliot implies is that change is not necessarily improvement unless informed by a proper respect for past wisdom; thus, where the curriculum is concerned, certain changes may well involve a desiccation rather than an enrichment. Some of these changes, for instance, have been antihistorical in kind—the current tendency to eliminate the study of the classical languages would be an example. However unsuitable the study of the classics may be for certain children, to eliminate from the schools a discipline concerned to such an extent with the fundamentals of our own civilization involves a great cultural loss. Those who see change as progress will tend to welcome the excision of what they regard as so much dead matter. Those who accept Eliot's view of cultural continuity and of the essential presentness of the past will deplore the loss.

The point is illustrated in an address Eliot made to the Classical Association in 1942, 'The Classics and the Man of Letters'. He speaks of the 'man of letters' rather than of the poet because he is concerned with the nurturing of talent rather than with the occasional writer of genius:

A Conservative Definition of Politics

. . . these secondary writers provide collectively, and individually in varying degrees, an important part of the environment of the great writer, as well as his first audience. . . .

As a rhetorical device in the lecture he queries the need to preserve a literature; but in the end he leaves us in no doubt as to its importance. His reason is a social one; a continuing concern for literature involves 'the preservation of developed speech, and of civilization against barbarism'. Themes are touched on which are more fully examined in *Notes Towards the Definition of Culture*, and which I can therefore ignore for the moment. What is immediately to the point is his stress on the importance of a common basis of education in the elaboration of a literature, and the fact that that common basis had been traditionally assumed by the classical languages and nurtured by the Christian faith:

> *. . . a new unity can only grow on the old roots: the Christian faith, and the classical languages which Europeans inherit in common. These roots are, I think, inextricably entwined.*[1]

Here, then, are the fundamentals of a tradition which Eliot proceeded to celebrate. The important implication, again, is that the individual mind is not enough; to produce a literature of any worth—and 'literature' can stand for any complex achievement of value—the social order must itself foster the individual growth. As he points out in another lecture, 'What is a Classic?'

> *A classic can only occur when a civilisation is mature; when a language and a literature are mature; and it must be the work of a mature mind. It is the importance of that civilisation and of that*

[1] 'The Classics and the Man of Letters', in *To Criticize the Critic* (London: Faber & Faber, 1965), p. 160.

> *language, as well as the comprehensiveness of the mind of the individual poet, which gives the universality. .... The maturity of a literature is the reflection of that of the society in which it is produced: an individual author—notably Shakespeare and Virgil—can do much to develop his language: but he cannot bring that language to maturity unless the work of his predecessors has prepared it for his final touch. A mature literature, therefore, has a history behind it . . . an ordered though unconscious progress of a language to realise its own potentialities within its own limitations.*

The lecture itself involves a prolonged analysis of how different states of society produced different types of maturity and immaturity in historically important literary figures.

Furthermore, if we accept Eliot's stress on the importance of the presentness of the past, and of its formative power on the maturing of the individual, we shall become suspicious of those views of education which see its function confined to the need to meet the challenge of change and the future. At present we tend to be moving from a view of education which saw its role as chiefly preservative of the values of the past to one which stresses its need to produce the flexibility of mind necessary to cope with a rapidly evolving situation. Paradoxically, what Eliot shows is that the mind which is imbued with the present significance of the past is the one best prepared to cope with the exigencies of change; he sees, in fact, no incompatibility between education as conservation and education as preparation for innovation. His conclusions about literacy creativeness again transcend their context: 'The persistence of literary creativeness in any people . . . consists in the maintenance of an unconscious balance between tradition in the larger sense . . .and the originality of the living generation'. The principle is of universal application; originality can only exist in a context, and that context is itself the creation of many past generations.

Fundamentals of an Organic Society

If one strand of the living tradition for Eliot was specifically literary, the other hinted at above, was derived from the historical Christian experience. Here was the positive belief, historically relevant to the long progress of our society, which could supersede the negativity of our liberalism and hence avoid on the one hand, a decline into apathy, or, on the other, a retreat into some form of totalitarianism:

> To those of us who can imagine, and are therefore repelled by, such a prospect, one can assert that the only possibility of control and balance is a religious control and balance; that the only hopeful course for a society which would thrive and continue its creative activity in the arts of civilisation is to become Christian. That prospect involves, at least, discipline, inconvenience and discomfort: but here as hereafter the alternative to hell is purgatory.[1]

Eliot then goes on to sketch the essential outlines of such a society. It involves the Christian state (the Christian Society 'under the aspect of legislation, public administration, legal tradition and form'), the Christian community (the totality of the society, of which one would expect a 'largely unconscious behaviour', where Christianity 'may be almost wholly realised in behaviour'), and the Community of Christians, from whom one would expect 'a conscious Christian life on its highest social level'. This view of society, with its hierarchy of levels, is of interest in Eliot's thought beyond its relevance to his views of a specifically Christian society. It divides the commonalty into those Eliot considers capable of consciousness, a comparatively small number, and those who, *whatever their social class*, are only capable of expressing their Christian

[1] *The Idea of a Christian Society* (London: Faber & Faber, 1939), pp. 23–4.

57

beliefs through their behaviour: the implication is that they lack the sustained intellectual capacity necessary to preserve their religious sentiments through conscious thought. His analysis of these two groups is so important that I must quote him at some length:

> *For the great majority of the people—and I am not here thinking of social classes, but of intellectual strata—religion must be primarily a matter of behaviour and habit, must be integrated with its social life, with its business and its pleasure; and the specifically religious emotions must be a kind of extension and sanctification of the domestic and social emotions. Even for the most highly developed and conscious individual, living in the world, a consciously Christian direction of thought and feeling can only occur at particular moments during the day and during the week, and these moments themselves recur in consequence of formed habits; to be conscious, without remission, of a Christian and a non-Christian alternative at moments of choice, imposes a very great strain. The mass of the population, in a Christian society, should not be exposed to a way of life in which there is too sharp and frequent a conflict between what is easy for them or what their circumstances dictate and what is Christian. The compulsion to live in such a way that Christian behaviour is only possible in a restricted number of situations, is a very powerful force against Christianity; for behaviour is as potent to affect belief, as belief to affect behaviour.*[1]

The notion, expressed a little later in the same chapter, that the 'religious life of the people would be largely a matter of behaviour and conformity,' and a further reference to the importance of the 'intellectual and spiritual superiority' of the Community of Christians, are at odds with modern egalitarian notions. The difference implied between the ordinary people and the superior class is defined in terms of levels of conscious-

---

[1] Ibid., p. 30.

ness: the majority acquire habitual patterns of behaviour within a Christian framework; the others consciously think through their Christian principles. Though Eliot wishes to promote some form of cultural unity, it is not one based on a similar level of conscious acceptance. The modern effort, on the other hand, is to posit an equal level of experiential submission. About his belief in the importance of some degree of unity there can be no doubt; continuity and coherence in politics, literature, and the arts must be assured, and this uniformity should be expressed

> . . . *in education by a settled, though not rigid agreement as to what everyone should know to some degree, and a positive distinction —however undemocratic it may sound—between the educated and the uneducated.*[1]

What he meant by this is perhaps more fully spelled out in 'The Classics and the Man of Letters'. Even among great writers there have been considerable differences in the level of their educational attainments. He cites John Bunyan and Abraham Lincoln as among those who have become great writers with very little educational advantage—they, like others, learned how to use the English language very largely from the Bible. So even where writers are concerned, it is not the amount of learning a man acquires that matters, but 'the type of education within which his schooling falls'. A common tradition of respect—in this case, for the ancients—is what matters more than the specific level of learning acquired.

Where the community at large is concerned, then, one may surmise that it is not important that all should have followed the same syllabus but that there should be a common respect for learning together with an assimilation of common assumptions at an appropriate level of awareness. The reference to

[1] Ibid., p. 40.

59

the formative power of the Bible is significant; one of the characteristic features of the Christian religion lies in its capacity to transmit a common mythology at very different levels of consciousness: either, for instance, iconographically or intellectually, to take the two extremes. Eliot does not ask that all should become theologians, although he does infer the acceptance of a common symbolism. Yet a religion has a power which is both emotional and intellectual, which all can assimilate at the appropriate level of response. In this way, society will become organic rather than mechanical. A combination of classicism and Christianity provides the common core of an appropriate common schooling—at one level it will manifest itself simply as story and parable; at another as exegesis and rational comment.

A nation's system of education is much more important than its system of government; only a proper system of education can unify the active and contemplative life, action and speculation, politics and the arts.[1]

Given such a common system of education and the common beliefs of Christianity, it should be possible to turn a people into a mutually interacting community and 'collectively to form the conscious mind and the conscience of the nation'.

THE CULTURAL ROLE OF ÉLITES

All this went with a constant sense of the inadequacy of the present situation—the effects of an 'unregulated industrialism', the feeling that our society is assembled around nothing more permanent 'than a congeries of banks, insurance companies and industries', and that it had no beliefs more essential

---

[1] Ibid., p. 41.

'than a belief in compound interest and the maintenance of dividends'. Eliot even went so far as to suggest that

> ... *without sentimentalising the life of the savage, we might practise the humility to observe, in some of the societies upon which we look down as primitive and backward, the operation of a social-religious-artistic complex which we should emulate upon a higher plane.*[1]

In one of the notes to the volume, Eliot predicts that the culture of the twentieth century will 'belong to the lower middle class as that of the Victorian age belonged to the upper middle class or commercial aristocracy'. By this he meant a society in which 'the standard man legislated for and catered for, the man whose passions must be manipulated, whose prejudices must be humoured, whose tastes must be gratified, will be the lower middle class one'[2]—a remark whose prescience can be confirmed in the current offerings of the mass media.

It is specifically to the problem of culture that he turns in his third and most important work of social criticism, *Notes Towards the Definition of Culture*. Here his concern is even more explicitly with the educative society, the one in which cultural creativity can blossom. The religious theme, though essentially present, is not as central as it is in the Idea. Religion has its place as an important prerequisite, but attention is focused on a wider ranging set of social and intellectual conditions—with particular reference to the educational ones—which are likely to nourish the individual sensibility.

Characteristically, all this appears under the guise of a perturbation about language; more specifically, about the outrage done in current discussion to the word 'culture'. Eliot is concerned about the essential conditions for the survival and

---

[1] Ibid., p. 62.
[2] Ibid., p. 78.

growth of a culture. Such concern may seem irrelevant in relation to other possible ends we may want society to attain; but he implies that if we do want a different form of society from the one he adumbrates, we had better cease paying lip service to culture.

He begins with the confident assertion that '. . . our own period is one of decline; that the standards of culture are lower than they were fifty years ago; and that the evidences of this decline are visible in every department of human activity'; but he also utters the warning that conditions favourable to a higher state of culture cannot be brought about by 'deliberate organisation'. The improvement we can look forward to is one in 'relatively minute particulars':

> *For if any definite conclusions emerge from this study, one of them is surely this, that culture is the one thing that we cannot deliberately aim at. It is the product of a variety of more or less harmonious activities, each pursued for its own sake: the artist must concentrate upon his canvas, the poet upon his typewriter, the civil servant upon the just settlement of particular problems as they present themselves upon his desk, each according to the situation in which he finds himself.*[1]

With this warning in mind, Eliot turns to an analysis of the manifestations of culture as they reveal themselves in the individual, the class, and the society, and as they manifest themselves in a variety of forms involving, for instance, manners, learning, 'philosophy' in its general sense, or the arts. As we are unlikely to find all these manifestations in one person, we can only find it in the pattern of society as a whole. Hence 'the culture of the individual cannot be isolated from that of the group, and . . . the culture of the group cannot be

[1] *Notes Towards the Definition of Culture* (London: Faber & Faber, 1948), p. 19.

abstracted from that of the whole society'.[1] Nevertheless, as society develops in functional complexity and increased specialization becomes necessary, different cultural levels also emerge. Such a process has its dangers: 'Cultural disintegration may ensue upon cultural specialisation'; and this is the 'most radical disintegration a society can suffer'. Its most serious manifestation lies in the division of culture and religion. For there is a sense in which the '. . . culture (is) essentially the incarnation (so to speak) of the religion of a people'— something which involves more than merely relationship, and yet something less than identification. Eliot, indeed, does not define very clearly the precise nature of the interrelationship, and admits that he only grasps it himself 'in flashes'. What he stresses is that religion and culture cannot remain indifferent to each other. Religion—even an inferior religion—'protects the mass of humanity from boredom and despair'; culture 'may even be described simply as that which makes life worth living'.[2]

Indeed, Eliot does here seem to confuse the descriptive and the prescriptive view of culture. It is at once that which is valuable ('makes life worth living') and yet includes

> . . . all the characteristic activities and interests of a people: Derby Day, Henley Regatta, the twelfth of August, a cup final, the dog races, the pin table, the dart board, Wensleydale cheese, boiled cabbage cut into sections, beetroot in vinegar, nineteenth-century Gothic churches and the music of Elgar.[3]

The fact that Eliot speaks of 'all the characteristic activities and interests of a people' would seem to preclude any suggestion that these activities are simply a selection of what makes

[1] Ibid., p. 24.
[2] Ibid., p. 37.
[3] Ibid., p. 31.

life worth living. This is the anthropologist's use of the word 'culture', not the Arnoldian. It is the Arnoldian conception, with its implication of selectivitiy, however, which lies behind his other view of culture as that which makes life worth living —otherwise his expression of such a view would simply involve the tautology that it is life which makes life worth living. And I think this confusion of the two uses of the word 'culture' arises out of Eliot's desire to maintain two propositions: that culture is not simply the property of a small section of society, but that all sections have things which help to make life worth living; and at the same time, that the culture of different sections of the population must manifest itself in different ways.

It is indeed the job of different *classes* in the community to maintain that part of the total culture which pertains peculiarly to them.

> *We have to try to keep in mind, that in a healthy society this maintainance of a particular level of culture is to the benefit, not merely of the class which maintains it, but of the society as a whole. Awareness of this fact will prevent us from supposing that the culture of a 'higher' class is something superfluous to society as a whole, or to the majority, and from supposing that it is something which ought to be shared equally by all other classes. It should also remind the 'higher' class, in so far as any such exists, that the survival of the culture in which it is particularly interested is dependent upon the health of the culture of the people.*[1]

This principle of the differentiation and yet the mutuality of culture is quite fundamental in Eliot's analysis. A healthy culture may be said to be 'common' at least to the extent that all are, in some degree, affected by every part of it. This means that no self-conscious minority can hope to preserve its own

[1] Ibid., p. 35.

level of culture in isolation from the rest of the society, as some, in despair at the vulgarity (as they have seen it) of modern popular culture have attempted to do; as he puts it, 'Fine art is the refinement, not the antithesis of popular art'. At the same time, no abandonment of the more self-conscious part of the culture in the name of democratic mingling will work either. The preservation of high cultural standards is not a luxury but a necessary condition of the cultural health of the whole society. At the same time this culture is only part of the culture of the society, which is the creation of the community as a whole, each class nourishing the rest. Hence the need for unity—and of differentiation within that unity.

But there was a further important condition, one that involved the preservation of classes as such. This is so contrary to modern tendencies toward the ideal of classlessness that Eliot's reasons must be examined with some care. And this necessitates a close study of his criticisms of the notion of the *élite*, which he considers will replace that of a class in the society of the future.

He sees that it is likely that former class distinctions will disappear and that the only distinctions of rank left will be those of implicit in the idea of *élites*, with perhaps some differentiation among the *élites* themselves. And this, while seeming to rectify the injustice of individuals accepting responsibilities for which their talents (or lack of them) do not equip them, has the further result of positing 'an atomic view of society'.

In drawing out what he considers to be the consequences of this position, Eliot is impelled to combat some of the views of the late Professor Karl Mannheim. In doing so, he develops his own view of the type of social structure which is necessary for cultural health. It involves the nature of the *élite* (as opposed to a number of *élites*) and the form of its relationship to the class structure:

> *. . . a growing weakness of our culture has been the increasing isola-*
> *tion of élites from each other, so that the political, the philosophical,*
> *the artistic, the scientific, are separated to the great loss of each of*
> *them, not merely through the arrest of any general circulation of*
> *ideas, but through the lack of those contracts and mutual influences*
> *at a less conscious level, which are perhaps even more important*
> *than ideas. The problem of the formation, preservation and develop-*
> *ment of the élites is therefore also the problem of the formation,*
> *preservation and development of the élite.*[1]

This *élite*, traditionally, has been associated with the upper, ruling class, some of whom have been very deficient in culture. Nevertheless, this class transmits standards of manners—what we might term 'breeding'—just as the *élite* associated with it preserves and, in the case of the more self-conscious members, creates the culture:

> *An élite must be attached to some class, whether higher or lower:*
> *but so long as there are classes at all it is likely to be the dominant*
> *class that attracts this élite to itself.*[2]

The point is that Eliot's view of the nature of a culture is a more organic one than that implicit in Mannheim. A culture is not to be identified with the sum of distinct cultural activities, at which one could arive by adding up the achievements of the different *élites*. This is because in any healthy culture there are unconscious as well as conscious elements; the culture of a particular tribe cannot be reduced to the sum of its details:

> *Understanding involves an area more extensive than that of which*
> *one can be conscious; one cannot be outside and inside at the same*
> *time.*[3]

[1] Ibid., p. 38.
[2] Ibid., p. 42.
[3] Ibid., p. 41.

A scientific understanding, he implies, is incomplete—the essence escapes; the only alternative is to live the culture, but then it can no longer be wholly captured for examination; the student will so identify himself with the people he is studying that he will no longer be able to bring the total pattern to consciousness.

The most important agency of cultural transmission is the family. Here the unconscious foundations of later cultural participation are laid; 'No man wholly escapes from the kind, or wholly surpasses the degree, of culture which he acquired from his early environment.' Furthermore, what Eliot has in mind is not the modern atomic family but one involving a bond over a longer period of time: 'A piety towards the dead, however obscure, and a solicitude for the unborn, however remote.' The class, then, represents a continuity of families involving at least the stabilization of manners, and providing a largely unconscious element of continuity (tradition) against which the *élite* can learn to refine itself. He contrasts this with the situation which might arise where *élites* existed independently of any attachment to a class system, a situation desired by many of his contemporaries. He points to the lack of any firm criterion by which we can recruit *élites* of the 'best' people, and suggests that any criterion imposed could have 'an oppressive effect on novelty'; and he queries the extent to which in such a society of *élites* apart from settled classes, education would be capable of transmitting the culture in any meaningful sense. He points out that the formation of a meritocracy will lead to the formation of groups of individuals

whose only common bond will be their professional interest: with no social cohesion, with no social continuity. They will be united only by a part, and that the most conscious part, of their personalities; they will meet like committees.[1]

[1] Ibid., p. 47.

The point of Eliot's insistence on the relevance of classes, as opposed to *élites*, is now becoming clearer. It is to ensure the transmission of the relevant part of the culture (relevant to the level of consciousness appropriate to the class concerned) in order to bring about cultural continuity, and hence traditions. He implies that in a culturally healthy state each section has its appropriate share in the total culture, some more, some less conscious, some more, some less specialized. This will be reflected also in the power structure, when a smaller group at a higher level will have equal power with a larger group at a lower level: for '. . . complete equality means universal irresponsibility. . . . A democracy in which everybody had an equal responsibility in everything would be oppressive for the conscientious and licentious for the rest.' The crux of the matter is stated here:

> *If we agree that the primary vehicle for the transmission of culture is the family, and if we agree that in a more highly civilised society there must be different levels of culture, then it follows that to ensure the transmission of the culture of these different levels there must be groups of families persisting, from generation to generation, each in the same way of life.*[1]

These, indeed, are his conditions of culture; though they will not necessarily ensure a high state of civilization, such a state is unlikely, he considers, to be found in their absence. For they involve the recognition of both unity and diversity—a 'common' culture manifested at a variety of levels of awareness; and they illustrate a point made at some length in the first chapter—Eliot's awareness of the necessity for some degree of tension (personal or social) for a higher degree of cultural activity:

[1] Ibid., p. 48.

The Cultural Role of Elites

*Neither a classless society, nor a society of strict and impenetrable
social barriers is good; each class should have constant additions and
defections; the classes, while remaining distinct, should be able to
mix freely; and they should all have a community of culture with
each other which will give them something in common, more fundamental than the community which each class has with its counterpart
in another society.*[1]

He continues to play with the tension of opposites; regionalism is to be encouraged as well as unity—it is to the cultural
advantage of the English that the Welsh and Scots and the
Irish should continue to assert a degree of independence and
thus, paradoxically, to enrich the English culture. Our development as individuals depends on our meeting opposition
as well as support. Some degree of friction, both between
individuals and between groups, is essential; it serves to work
off aggressiveness; and it produces creative results:

*Numerous cross-divisions favour peace within a nation, by dis-
persing and confusing animosities; they favour peace within nations,
by giving every man enough antagonism at home to exercise all his
aggressiveness.*[2]

This need for diversity as well as unity makes the idea of a
world culture inadmissible ... it would involve a dehumaniza-
tion of humanity, and it would in any case encounter the incompatibility of different religions and thus prove an impossibility. At the same time, as the interplay of cultures must
to some degree be a good thing, we cannot totally abandon the
idea of a world culture, while granting its practical impossibility.

Tension should exist, even in the relationship between

[1] Ibid., p. 50.
[2] Ibid., p. 60.

69

Church and State. Yet Christendom should be one. Within such a unity, however, there should be a persistent conflict:

> ... *The local temperament must express its particularity in its form of Christianity, and so must the social stratum, so that the culture proper to each area and each class may flourish; but there must also be a force holding these areas and these classes together.*[1]

A RESTRICTED DEMOCRACY

Before I turn to a consideration of the role assigned to education in a culturally revived social order, it would be well to draw together and critically examine Eliot's views on society. He looks at it in the light of his experience as a poet and as a Christian—from the standpoint that is, of both culture and religion. He notes that both grow from the same roots, but that, with social development, both diverge and can even become antagonistic. It is, however, this twin standpoint that leads him to diagnose the ills of our present society, its deficiency in culture. It is lacking in belief because it is wormeaten with liberalism, a creed serving to release energy without providing forms by which such energy can aim toward some positive affirmations. We are therefore threatened with boredom and purposelessness. It is deficient in culture because the disintegration of the agencies for the transmission of culture—notably the family and the separate classes in the community from which the family draws its strength and stability—has produced an atomic state of society in which men no longer meet in terms of common if diverse values. At the same time, Eliot does not suggest as a solution the disappearance of these characteristics of our present society, but their being counterbalanced by other forces; both liberalism and social mobility have essential roles to play in a revitalized society and culture.

[1] Ibid., p. 82.

Nevertheless, these characteristics need to be brought into a state of fruitful tension with their opposite—liberalism with a state of strong belief, social mobility with the persistence of classes. This is perhaps the most remarkable feature of Eliot's views, in contradistinction to the root and branch extirpations which are the usual recourse of social critics. At the heart of his solution lies the need for both freedom and order, so as to avoid either petrifaction and deliquescence.

Thus, Eliot's ideas cannot simply be dismissed as reactionary; such a rejection would miss the revolutionary elements which are clearly part of his thinking. He does not see the mass of people as subjects simply for manipulation, even if for their own good, but as essential participants in any culturally healthy state of society. Again he avoids the sentimentality of those who seek salvation in the working classes, because he sees that their participation must in some degree be an unselfconscious one, arising from good habits rather than from overt contribution. This is to mingle acceptance with realism—an awareness of deficiencies of consciousness combined with an understanding of a need for an organic role. Thus, he steered a central path between sentimentality and brutality.

Furthermore, by taking culture as his interpretative concept rather than politics, his viewpoint is more extensive than is normal among social theorists. He sees that politics is only one factor in a whole cultural complex and that there are other satisfactions of living than those involved in the extension of the franchise or the securing of 'rights'. It is true that his conception of culture remains implicit rather than explicit, that he is liable to confuse the anthropological and the prescriptive senses, and that this confusion causes some difficulties. As it is never altogether clear precisely what makes life worth living, it is never apparent how people who might lack these amenities —those to whom we commonly refer today as the underprivileged—are to be afforded an opportunity to make good their deficiencies. Like many social theorists, Eliot does not define how, out of the actual, the ideal is to appear—for, in fact, the ideal is his greatest concern. To be fair to him, he does indicate that he simply wishes to state the conditions of culture, not necessarily to recommend their attainment; but it is hard to avoid the suggestion that he would indeed want to make life worth living for us.

Furthermore, there is one great deficiency which, unconsciously, runs all through his talk about culture. He fails to include the most characteristic feature of the culture of his times—scientific culture. Had he devoted more attention to scientific culture, he might have seen more fully how some *élites* can function and interact in the modern world without a felt need to define closely the nature and extent of their contact with one another. His omission can be illustrated by the fact that when he speaks of the way in which people within an *élite* group communicate with each other, he has in mind a particular range of linguistic communications. What he is saying is that the members of an *élite* should not meet together as if they were simply members of a committee—they should participate at a deeper level which includes an unconscious awareness of common assumptions as well as overt communication: they must, that is to say, continually live their culture as well as be conscious of it. It is worth considering his description of this process at length:

The élite should be something different, something much more organically composed, than a panel of bonzes, caciques and tycoons. Men who meet only for definite serious purposes, and on official occasions, do not wholly meet. They may have some common concern very much at heart; they may, in the course of repeated contacts, come to share a vocabulary and an idiom which appear to communicate every shade of meaning necessary for their common purpose; but they will continue to retire from these encounters each to his private social world as well as to his solitary world. Everyone has observed that the possibilities of contented silence, of a mutual happy awareness when engaged upon a common task, or an underlying seriousness and significance in the enjoyment of a silly joke, are characteristics of any close personal intimacy; and the congeniality of any circle of friends depends upon a common social convention, a common ritual, and common pleasure of relaxation. These aids to intimacy are no less important for the communication of meaning in words, than the possession of a common subject upon which the several parties are informed.[1]

It is clear that the intimacies Eliot has in mind are intended to inform the meanings implicit in overt verbal communication. But such intimacies can only have relevance where language is specifically capable of ambiguity; and the function of such intimacies is to resolve ambiguities at an unconscious level. In discourse where meaning is unequivocal these intimacies can play no part. And of course, such ambiguity, such openness to the possibilities of nuance, is characteristic only of that type of discourse of which literature forms the paradigm. Scientific discourse is unequivocal in meaning; it depends on usages whose conventions are clear and unambiguous, often involving signs or symbols whose meaning is quite arbitrarily fixed by convention. Eliot's concern with literary usages where language shows the effect of its long involvement with the habits and behaviour of men blinds him to the unambiguity of the language of science and mathematics.

As a result he failed to appreciate that many of the *élites* are able to work together in terms of their technical competences. The unambiguous language in which these competences are expressed gives an impression of mutuality, of

[1] Ibid., p. 85.

common understanding which, in fact, only exists in terms of their expertise and associated issues and leaves untouched many other areas of contact. Eliot said that the *élites* today meet like committees; but, of course, this is precisely how a great deal of the business of the modern world is transacted. The issue at stake and not the fundamental values of the participant holds the forefront of attention. In coming to an agreement in relation to the items of the agenda, it is customary to ignore the deeper cleavages in order to arrive at some form of consensus. The folkways of committees have indeed evolved largely to plaster over the disagreements arising from differences of background and conflicting notions of relative values. Here, indeed, Eliot is not altogether correct to suggest that liberalism has induced a spirit of toleration; it is a creed precisely suited to the positive work of committees. It means that no man is prepared to push his point of view to the extent of rupture. Whatever divisions, indeed animosities, lurk below the surface, the usual outcome is the presentation of the agreed formula.

Thus, given the 'negative capability' of committees, the positive work of a society largely run by committees as ours is, becomes possible. But at a profounder level, Eliot is right. Most of what issues from the deliberations of committees is inescapably banal and insupportable to someone, like Eliot, who is concerned to face up to what he considers to be the basic dilemmas of the human being. The modern world pays heavy price for its willingness to be fobbed off by glib formulas and the emasculated language of committee reports. Education is a case in point. This dissatisfaction one feels with many of the voluminous reports which have appeared in England in recent years lies in their unwillingness to tackle fundamental issues. The Robbins Report, for instance, never asks what all the suggested proliferation of higher education is *for*. Out of its thousands of pages, it devotes exactly one and a half to a discussion of aims; those who wish to know what it is all about have to read between the lines. For inevitably, of course, values are involved; if they are not explicitly argued, they will reveal themselves implicitly—and will often be all the cruder for not having been overtly argued. The requirements of consensus exact a heavy price in terms of fuzzy and unrewarding purposes. The lack of astringency reveals itself in the muddied, lifeless prose in which these reports are inevitably couched. Good prose, as Eliot himself remarked, cannot be written by people who lack real convictions.

Yet, his view of some sections of this 'people' is not altogether justified. In the face of the vast sentimentality which surrounds current talk and discussion about ordinary people in the modern world, his references to the 'mob' provide a welcome corrective. And it must be understood that by 'mob' he was not simply referring to the lower classes, the traditional attribution of the word. His judgment was a qualitative one which applied to the total society, not one which accepted current class divisions: I have heard him express profound contempt for business men and politicians in terms which would lead one to expect their inclusion in the category of 'mob'. In any case, those he alluded to as the 'mob' were as much the victims as the creators of unfavourable social circumstances. They were being asked by modern conditions to develop a degree of consciousness which in general he considered was beyond them; but as an alternative what Eliot had to offer them was nothing more sustaining than habit, traditional behaviour patterns. In this he revealed much less understanding of human possibilities than did his contemporary, D. H. Lawrence. Lawrence, too, strongly deprecated the universal development of consciousness; but his intimate knowledge of working people as well as of other classes of the community enabled him to suggest different possibilities for ordinary people. Knowledge for them, he states, was to be 'mythical, symbolic, dynamic', which suggests a much more positive orientation. He had noted in his own experience the real delights of the people, their capacity for intimacy and forms of sensuous apprehension which opened up creative possibilities far beyond Eliot's recommendation of habit as the ruling force of their lives. The difference is partly explained by the fact that, although both writers were moralists, Eliot, as had been pointed out, existed within the traditional framework, while Lawrence burst out of it. Eliot in general sees the restrictive though creative power of regularity; Lawrence places greater emphasis on involvement in the immediate and newly given. Lawrence, too, had more intimate acquaintance with the working classes than Eliot.

Nevertheless, Eliot's analysis of the dilemmas of consciousness is of great importance. He realizes that people are becoming increasingly self-conscious. Partly this has been encouraged by the growth of scepticism which has characterized the development of our civilization; it has manifested itself, in Eliot's words, as 'the habit of examining evidence and the capacity for delayed decision'. Part of this capacity for delay reveals itself in an ability to transcend immediate self-interest and to reason about the desires of the self in a larger context. The effect of this has been, in many instances, to inhibit action; life has become an endless succession of problems, each a burden to the action of the self:

> ... *in the world to-day we find ourselves more and more consciously trying to manipulate what has been left to take its own course—that is, our area of conscious manipulation becomes bigger and bigger. A problem comes into existence through our ability to become aware of it; the awareness shapes the problem; and once we are conscious*

of a problem, we cannot dismiss it from consciousness; we find ourselves under obligation to try to find an answer.[1]

This proliferation of 'problems' confronted many people with an area and range of decision making which was exhausting to sustain; 'We must remember', Eliot said, 'that being more conscious about everything is a very great strain.' As a counterbalance, then, to this insistence on consciousness, Eliot takes pains to insist on the importance of unconscious harmonies and acceptances. His references to traditional pieties and loyalties, his stress on habit, and his feeling that a community needs to restrict the areas of possible disagreement indicate his concern. Creative though an element of friction may be, if too wide an area of behaviour is laid open to contentious disagreement the forces holding together a community may be threatened; the centrifugal forces within a society must be balanced by the centripetal forces, for otherwise controversy itself becomes futile:

It can only be usefully practiced where there is common understanding. It requires common assumptions; and perhaps the assumptions that are only felt are more important than those that can be formulated. The acrimony which accompanies much debate is a symptom of differences so large that there is nothing to argue about. We experience such profound differences with some of our contemporaries, that the nearest parallel is the difference between the mentality of one epoch and another.[2]

Though he deprecated the overstimulation of consciousness in the minds of many members of the community, he was not an enemy of democracy. He realized that the notion of de-

[1] 'The Aims of Education', in *To Criticize the Critic* (London: Faber & Faber, 1965), p. 94.
[2] *After Strange Gods*, op. cit., p. 13.

mocracy, as a result of constant usage in a wide variety of contexts and with reference to a wide variety of political systems, had become almost void of content. Nevertheless, he opposed deriding the notion:

> *It is one thing to say, which is sadly certain, that democratic govern-*
> *ment has been watered down to nothing. It is one thing to say, which*
> *is equally sad and certain, that from the moment when the suffrage*
> *is conceived as a right instead of as a privilege and a duty and a*
> *responsibility, we are on the way merely to government by an in-*
> *visible oligarchy instead of government by a visible one. But it is*
> *another thing to ridicule the idea of democracy. A real democracy*
> *is always a restricted democracy. and can flourish with some limita-*
> *tion by hereditary rights and responsibilities.*

Certainly, he was no believer in equality; he once said to me, 'You can have equality; you can have culture; but you cannot have both.' But he accepted the idea that one of the aims of education was to enable people to play their parts as citizens of a democracy, though in terms which implied participation in his own 'restricted' version.

CULTURE VERSUS POLITICS

Perhaps Eliot's most valuable contribution as a social theorist is the standpoint from which he comments on current problems and suggests possible prescriptions. His method is analytical rather than hortatory—the tone is cool and dispassionate but not without astringency. He contributes to a debate rather than lays down the law: his attitude is that if we want a flourishing culture, we need to consider the conditions under which a high state of civilization can thrive, because such conditions do not exist at the moment. He considers his purpose an important one in a world where the traditional categories of social and political discussion are in terms of 'rights', 'obligations', 'authority', and the like. Not that such concepts are not important, but their use is subordinate to the wider purpose of cultural well-being. Such well-being, in so far as it penetrates the lives of all at a variety of levels and forms the inescapable texture of their lives, represents a profounder problem than that of voting rights or political functioning. And it represents an approach which sets educational problems in their rightful context—a cultural, not a political one. For education touches on many more facets of the personality than those implicit in making political decisions. As Eliot himself puts it, 'The desire to vote always for the right candidate cannot become the ambition of a lifetime'.

3

On Education

THE ROLE OF EDUCATION IN FOSTERING CULTURE

It is similarly a difference of perspective which makes Eliot's specific comments on education so valuable. In recent years our thinking about education has been dominated by political necessities and social theorizing; we have been much concerned with problems arising out of the class structure, a desire for social justice, and the state of the economy—the three concerns have, of course, been interrelated. Eliot's interest in education derived from a different set of priorities. To him education was a cultural manifestation, and he was interested in the part it could play in the development of a culturally healthy society. I have already noted that his general social approach was deeply imbued with his specific discipline as a poet; just as his creative enterprise made him suspicious of socio-political abstractions (he reminds us that Henry James had so fine a mind that it was never violated by an *idea*), so it also brought home to him the need for the educative rather than the functional society. Furthermore, his poetry was essentially the product of a sophisticated mind, one which had undergone an extensive period of education and yet was sufficiently detached from its academic education to be able to reflect on the benefits—and otherwise—it had derived.

I have, perhaps, adequately stressed the interrelatedness of the poet, the social theorist, and the educationist; nevertheless, reiteration is not without point. For all three manifestations are primarily the products of a mind which is itself educated—to an extent, indeed, that is uncommon among professional educationists, those who teach education as a field of study. 'Education' as a meeting point of university disciplines is still sufficiently in its infancy to make the insights of the amateur, though educated mind significant for its procedures. Perhaps it always will be, because underlying the discovery of specific fact—which is often a technical matter of some complexity—is the value judgment as to which investigation has relevance or priority. And such judgments must always be open to the opinions and arguments of distinguished minds. It is often argued that there are no experts in values, that in a democratic society every man has a right to an opinion and a right to have that opinion treated with respect. The former proposition about right to an opinion one can concede, the latter is more questionable. At least, achievement in other relevant fields must create some sort of presumption to a special fitness, especially achievement in a field like literature where value considerations are central to the activity.

Furthermore, in Eliot's case, we are dealing with a mind which was highly self-consciously aware of the role of education in his own achievement. Rousseau said of Plato's *Republic* that it was not so much a treatise on politics as on education. Similarly, Eliot, as I hope has been revealed in this book, was concerned in his social theorizing not so much with the traditional problems of political philosophy—the role of authority and the nature of the state—but with the formation of a vital and culturally alive community. His 'authority' is not adumbrated in terms of the role of kingship, or the balance of the legislative and the executive, but with the more intangible forces of cultural continuity and the heritage of the past in revivifying the present. His assumed picture of man is not of

81

the voter or the representative of the general will, but the person of positive and creative energies starved of emotional satisfactions in the vacuity of current belief and the emptiness of contemporary values.

I have drawn attention to the combination of scepticism and affirmation which marked Eliot's social theorizing. We find the same qualities in his specifically educational views, the same ambivalence, the same awareness of ambiguity and paradox. He was a learned and highly educated man, aware that the tradition he valued had to be obtained 'by great labour'; yet he could see that education was not necessarily an unequivocal benefit. In speaking of Blake, for instance, he realized that there was a certain advantage in the fact that Blake 'was not compelled to acquire any other education in literature than he wanted, or to acquire it for any other reason than that he wanted it'. Eliot, however, was not positing any romantic view of the untutored poet. He appreciated that:

> It is important that the artist should be highly educated in his own art; but his education is one that is hindered rather than helped by the ordinary processes of society which constitute education for the ordinary man. For these processes consist largely in the acquisition of impersonal ideas which obscure what we really are and feel, what we really want, and what really excites our interest. It is of course not the actual information acquired, but the conformity which the accumulation of knowledge is apt to impose, that is harmful.[1]

Yet again there is a paradox in his view of the functioning of the poetic impulse. 'What we really are and feel' refers only to one aspect of the creative role. Learning to be a poet (by which is implied learning in any profound meaningful sense) is only in part a voyage in self discovery. For once the 'true' self has

---

[1] Essay on William Blake in *Selected Essays*.

been uncovered, it is not the self that seems to matter, it is the learning. We have already noted Eliot's reaction against individuality, personality, idiosyncrasy, eccentricity; in the act of creation it is not a self which is revealed, but a work which is performed. To the resolution and implication of this paradox I must address myself, for it is a matter of considerable importance at a time when the notion of 'creativity' plays so crucial a role in current educational theorizing.

The emphasis on 'what we are and feel' is conventional romantic doctrine, part of the cult of sincerity, of uncovering the 'real' self under the accretions which social convention has laid on it. Nevertheless, there is an element of fraud in this concern for the 'real' self, as if it were something apart from social process—because the 'self' is, in large measure, the creation of society. The language which it uses, the habits it acquires, its characteristic poses and stances are inevitably socially conditioned. Even the reaction against convention itself becomes a convention, as the most superficial study of modern life indicates. When, therefore, Eliot emphasizes that 'the emotion of art is impersonal', that

> *What happens (to the poet in the act of creation) is a continual surrender of himself as he is at the moment to something which is more valuable. The progress of an artist is a continual self-sacrifice, a continual self extinction of personality. . . .*[1]

He is not denying the element of 'what we are and feel'; he is placing the stress on the other element in the creative act—the making, the product. He is making it clear that the poet assumes a role, a 'mask', to use a word from one of his contemporaries, William Butler Yeats. He is performing a social act of communication, and therefore needs to concentrate on

[1] From 'Tradition and the Individual Talent'.

the act rather than on the feeling behind the act. A poet, he considered, has not a ' "personality" to express, but a particular medium, which is only a medium and not a personality'. Therefore, he considers, 'Impressions and experiences which are important for the man may take no place in the poetry, and those which take place in the poetry may play quite a negligible part in the man, the personality.'

Psychologically it rings very true. Even writing what I am writing now—essentially an act of re-creation, certainly not of creation—involves at very least a self which is different from the self of everyday experiences, of eating breakfast or lazing in the garden; one is even conscious of resistance from this other self in one's concentrated effort to see the object of one's discourse (T. S. Eliot) as in himself he really was. At the very least one assumes another self, choosing one's words, checking one's expression, striving to encompass the task. In a sense my version of Eliot's thought is as I see him; but in seeing him I bring into play a critical sense where the controlling factor is something other than myself—the words which are Eliot's —and a self which is often at odds with the self which prefers to laze and sunbathe.

Thus one sees the relevance of Eliot's emphasis on 'impersonality' and of Yeats's unintentional gloss on it:

> *I think that all happiness depends on the energy to assume the mask of some other self; that all joyous or creative life is a re-birth as something not oneself, something which has no memory and is created in a moment and perpetually renewed.*

Thus we should regard with some suspicion notions that associate creation with self-expression; at the very least it makes sense to ask 'which self?' The term is indeed either tautologous (what else could one express?) or misleading (one expresses

84

something other than the self, because one is concerned to say *something*, and provided that something is communicable at all, it belongs to the public not the private world).

But there is another element of passivity, of waiting on the event:

> *Consequently, we must believe that 'emotion recollected in tran-
> quillity' is an inexact formula. For it is neither emotion, nor recollec-
> tion, nor, without distortion of meaning, tranquillity. It is a concen-
> tration, and a new thing resulting from the concentration, of a very
> great number of experiences which to the practical and active person
> would not seem to be experiences at all; it is a concentration which
> does not happen consciously or of deliberation. These experiences are
> not 'recollected', and they finally unite in an atmosphere which is
> 'tranquil' only in that it is a passive attending upon the event.*[1]

This is simply another way of saying that creativity cannot emerge simply from an act of will. Of course, Eliot realized that there was much in the writing of poetry which must be 'conscious and deliberate'; but simply to rely on the desire to create, as something to be willed and achieved, was insufficient.

The point is that creativity of significance is the by-product of something other than itself—either at the personal, or in-deed, at the social level. It is the having something to say rather than the search to say something which matters. One of the reasons why much writing of poetry fails is because it strives too consciously for '. . . new emotions to express; and in this search for novelty in the wrong place it discovers the perverse'. In the same way, a culture cannot consciously be created. A culture, in fact, is the sum total of the activities of a society; it is not something that can be planned by some central committee for 'culture is the one thing that we cannot deliberately aim at'. The reason becomes clear: 'Culture can

[1] Ibid.

never be wholly conscious—there is always more to it than we are conscious of; and it cannot be planned because it is also the unconscious background of all our planning.'

This is to say in other terms that we cannot be wholly conscious of ourselves and that there is a sense in which our highest endeavours are doomed to imperfection. What, then, are we to say of a cultural *organization*, our system of education, which consciously seeks to foster and improve the quality of life of our people? Here at least is the exercise of the conscious will. Yet for all this overt effort we have to face the possibility that Eliot is right when he asserts, '. . . with some confidence that our own period is one of decline'; I would quarrel with his view that this decline is 'visible in every department of human activity'—the decline, though real, has, it seems to me, been unevenly spread. Nevertheless, with the transmission of this culture being one of the major purposes of education, the situation is, at first sight, perplexing.

A key is perhaps provided in Eliot's gloss on a statement published in a volume connected with an Oxford conference on Church, Community, and State (1937):

> *The purpose of education, it seems, is to transmit culture: so culture (which has not been defined) is likely to be limited to what can be transmitted by education.*[1]

The crux of the matter lies in the form of transmission. Though Eliot does not put it in this way, one can see what, from his point of view, would be wrong with educational transmission in the form practised in the schools; it would fail to transmit those vital unconscious elements which can only be transferred within a social unit closer and more unified

[1] *Notes Towards the Definition of Culture* (London: Faber & Faber, 1948), p. 96.

in spirit than that of the ordinary school. We now see why he considered the primary agent of cultural transmission to be the family, because only in an atmosphere of that degree of intimacy would fundamental feelings and attitudes be transmitted. The fact is that the school as a separate institution is too remote from the real pressures of living to affect profoundly the lives of many of its inhabitants. Eliot's realization of this is clearly behind his appreciation that the schooling we impose is an 'abstraction', and that it is possible that 'facility of education will lead to indifference to it'. That it has become an abstraction is illustrated by the habit we have of referring to the 'half-educated':

> *In earlier ages the majority could not be said to have been 'half-educated' or less: people had the education necessary for the functions they were called upon to perform. It would be incorrect to refer to a member of a primitive society, or to a skilled agricultural labourer in any age, as half-educated or quarter-educated or educated to any smaller fraction. Education in the modern sense implies a disintegrated society, in which it has come to be assumed that there must be one measure of education according to which everyone is educated simply more or less. Hence* Education *has become an abstraction.*[1]

Indeed, to assert that our schools can pass on our culture is to assert that 'an organ is a whole organism':

> *For the schools can transmit only a part, and they can only transmit this part effectively, if the outside influences, not only of family and environment, but of work and play, of newsprint and spectacles and entertainment and sport, are in harmony with them.*[2]

[1] Ibid., p. 105.
[2] Ibid., p. 106.

Thus we have come to expect that our educational institutions will 'do for society what society ought to do for itself'. They are indeed institutions which are at once highly organized and formless. As a result 'We can easily aim at more and accomplish less, than our grandparents did'.

Here, it seems to me, we have the most convincing reason to explain the comparative failure of our educational system— a failure which is almost complete with at least some sections of the school population. It is attempting an impossible task. One might go further and say that by institutionalizing the transmission of our serious culture in this way, we may be doing an actual harm to our standards. We are suggesting that 'culture' is something that belongs to the schoolroom and not to our everyday life; we too often invoke the will rather than the sensibilities, and we try to transmit the same level of culture to the total population. And this last possibility raises very fundamental and vital issues for our age which Eliot again does a good deal to illumine.

I have already drawn attention in the last chapter to the way in which Eliot divides the Christian community from the community of Christians. The operative distinction, as was pointed out, is between levels of consciousness, between those who must rely on habit and those who can work out their principles on an intellectual basis. This distinction also runs throughout his educational thought. All need a common background of assumption to promote the unity of the community; but not all can participate at a conscious level in the same culture. And to attempt to do so is to 'adulterate and cheapen what you give':

To treat the 'uneducated' mass of the population as we might treat some innocent tribe of savages to whom we are impelled to deliver the true faith is to encourage them to neglect or despise that culture

*which they should possess and from which the more conscious part
of culture draws vitality; and to aim to make everyone share in the
appreciation of the fruits of the more conscious part of culture is to
adulterate and cheapen what you give.*[1]

The clearest instance of this occurs in those former colonial
nations which have taken over so completely the culture of
their former masters that they have come to despise their own
indigenous culture. The spectacle of African children following the set pattern of grammar school or *lycée*, not because
what they learn has any relevance to their lives or ways of
thinking but purely for reasons of prestige, is at once sadden-
ing and ludicrous—and diseducative. This is commonly appreciated. What is not so frequently accepted is that in England
something of the same process is taking place. Sufficient work
has been done by sociologists to indicate, for instance, that
many sections of the working-class population have different
traditions of behaviour, different ethical views, even a different
speech, from that of other sections of the community. But the
notion of different levels of consciousness appropriate to different sections of the community is unacceptable to the unifying tendencies of a collectivist society and, ideologically, to our
notions of social justice. Of course, the situation is complicated
by the fact that many children from what are termed 'culturally deprived homes' (by which is usually meant that they are
deprived of a certain *sort* of culture) are capable of a higher
level of conscious response than they have been offered in the
past. The other problem they pose arises out of the nature of
an industrial society and relates to the work that many of them
are going to be asked to do. To condemn human beings to the
type of uncreative, repetitive work that so many are con-
demned to despite the onset of automation, without making

[1] Ibid., p. 106.

some attempt to provide satisfactions beyond the pay packet is naturally repellent to humanitarian consciences. Furthermore, the erosion of the traditional folk culture which was centred in large measure around pre-industrial work patterns and their challenge to skill and aptitude, means that the current representatives of the folk have little to fall back on but the cheaper forms of mass media offerings. The great rot at the heart of modern civilization—a form of fungoid growth at least as threatening as the atomic bomb, and more likely to effect its consequences—is the emotional debility and falsification this situation is likely to encourage.

There is, indeed, something much more honest in Eliot's comment on reasons for raising the school leaving age than is usual in arguments addressed to this end:

> . . . *instead of affirming what is to be doubted, that everyone will profit by as many years of tuition as we can give him, admit that the conditions of life in modern industrial society are so deplorable, and the moral restraints so weak, that we must prolong the schooling of young people simply because we are at our wits' end to know what to do to save them.*[1]

The mixture of realism and concern is indeed interesting. 'Saving' people is out of favour and will bring a ready sneer from some who pretend to be 'on the side' of young people. There is probably nothing to be said to them; those less prejudiced in favour of modern permissiveness will note the concept as an interesting example of Eliot's moral involvement in the diagnosis he seems at times so detachedly to offer.

Furthermore, there is no doubt but that the increased concern for consciousness raises profound issues for our system of schooling. For, in the attempt to spread the highest con-

[1] Ibid., p. 104.

sciousness to all, we run the grave risk of adulterating and degrading our culture:

> *For there is no doubt that in our headlong rush to educate everybody, we are lowering our standards, and more and more abandoning the study of those subjects by which the essentials of our culture—of that part of it which is transmissible by education—are transmitted; destroying our ancient edifices to make ready the ground upon which the barbarian nomads of the future will encamp in their mechanised caravans.*[1]

Even in this outburst ('an incidental flourish to relieve the feelings of the writer') one recognizes both the justice and the prescience. The current student revolt is not only political (the desire for 'representation' wherever representation would be appropriate) but also, in important areas, cultural—the rejection of the traditional moral and intellectual restraints which have gone to make up the culture of the West.

> *A 'mass-culture' will always be a substitute-culture; and sooner or later the deception will become apparent to the more intelligent of those upon whom culture has been palmed off.*[2]

The causes of student 'unrest' are no doubt complex. It is not unreasonable to suggest, however, that one discontent arises out of alienation from subject-matter of which certain people just cannot make sense; another, more sophisticated, disillusionment springs from those who, making sense, find what is offered wanting in the terms in which it is offered—as examination fodder.

The conclusion, which our age finds so unpalatable, is that

[1] Ibid., p. 108.
[2] Ibid., p. 107.

On Education

. . . it is an essential condition of the preservation of the quality of the culture of the minority, that it should continue to be a minority culture.[1]

As he puts it elsewhere, 'The development of culture does not mean bringing everybody up to the front, which amounts to no more than making everyone keep in step.' Or, to repeat another remark equally unpalatable: 'You can have equality; you can have culture, but you cannot have both.' (I take it that here he was equating 'culture' with the more self-conscious aspects of culture.) The gradual but accelerating erosion of 'minority' culture under the impact of popular cultural activities, the betrayal by the 'minority' of their heritage and responsibilities everywhere apparent in the established organs of communication so characteristic of our technically advanced society, serve to illustrate the accuracy of Eliot's diagnosis. Not the least of our debts to him lies in the extent to which he has kept us aware of a tradition which, whatever its weaknesses, allows us to judge the degradation of our times.

At the same time, he shares the belief with Plato that ordinary people best attain their own excellence—their culture— through the development of tastes and character by force of habit. I must expand here a little what I have said about this in the last chapter. Conscious that 'behaviour is also belief', and that even those most born to consciousness 'live also at the level on which belief and behaviour cannot be distinguished', he saw that modern industry and the educational agencies relevant to it needed to engage people at a deeper level than that represented by the repetitive process and the pay packet in order to exercise any cultural effectiveness or to play any educative role in the lives of its operatives. He saw that the old form of apprenticeship to a craft engaged much

[1] Ibid., p. 107.

more of the participant's personality than does the technical school:

> ... *the apprentice (ideally, at least) did not merely serve his master, and did not merely learn from him as one would learn at a technical school—he became assimilated into a way of life which went with that particular trade or craft; and perhaps the lost secret of the craft is this, that not merely a skill but an entire way of life was transmitted.*[1]

Eliot concurred with Miss Marjorie Reeves in wishing the worker to take an active intellectual interest in the industry in which he was employed, and further advised that 'An industry if it is to engage more than the conscious mind of the worker, should also have a way of life somewhat peculiar to its initiates, with its own forms of festivity and observances.'

The notion, then, that even current education is a panacea for our ills receives a wide shock at Eliot's hands. And this should go a long way to lower the emotional tone of some of our contemporary discussions on education. If education is too easily accessible, indeed, indifference to it may occur: 'A high average of general education is perhaps less necessary for a civil society than a respect for learning.' Other of the favourite shibboleths of our times receive rough treatment at Eliot's hands. The notion of equality of opportunity can be pushed to undesirable extremes. Whereas the exceptional individual should have means by which his talents will receive the necessary stimulus,

> ... *the ideal of an educational system which would automatically sort out everyone according to his native capacities is unattainable in practice; and if we made it our chief aim, would disorganise society and debase education. It would disorganise society, by sub-*

[1] Ibid., p. 43.

93

stituting for classes, élites of brains, or perhaps only of sharp wits.
. . . The prospect of a society ruled and directed only by those who
have passed certain examinations or satisfied tests devised by psycho-
logists is not reassuring.[1]

He does not, in any case, believe in the Mute Inglorious Mil-
ton dogma, the belief, that is, that there is a reservoir of the
highly talented only waiting to be tapped by our educational
system. Even if it were based on fact, the neglect of the principle might well be compensated for by our avoiding 'some
Cromwell *guilty* of his country's blood'. And he sees that envy
has played its part in the current emphasis on equality of
opportunity.

So we have the paradox of the learned poet, one who himself
had undergone one of the most intensive *formal* educations
that the modern world can offer, preserving a cool scepticism
before the developing claims of the system of which he remains a major beneficiary. Paradoxically, it is his very respect
for that education and his detached appraisal of what its attainment had cost him that, in part, made him sceptical of current
pressures. Education, he realized 'deteriorate it as you may . . .
is still going to demand a good deal of drudgery'; and he was
not prepared to accept the polite fiction that the community
as a whole had either the ability or the application to under-
take the drudgery. It was partly because he was so deeply
appreciative of the importance of education that he realized
that what could be transmitted by a Ministry of Education
was limited in incidence and scope; and it is precisely because
he was both disinterested and learned that his realization of
this fact is of such profound significance. *Notes Towards the*
Definition of Culture was not written as a social or political
polemic, was not a weapon in a developing political fracas. It

[1] Ibid., p. 101.

contains the ruminations, at once remote and yet involved, of a man who has tried to make sense of his own personal world and of the effort that has gone to its creation. As a prelude to his Introduction to the book he quotes a remark by Lord Acton: 'I think our studies ought to be all but purposeless. They want to be pursued with chastity like mathematics.' When we have finished reading what he has to say, the force of the quotation comes home to us. Part of the value of his reflections lies in their lack of any overt design upon us; what we are offered is an argument, not a programme. Yet as chastity (*pace* the modern world) is a positive state, so the outcome of the argument is a positive illumination. There could hardly be a better example of Eliot's own injunction, in *Murder in the Cathedral*, that we should 'learn to care and not to care'.

THE AIMS OF EDUCATION

In the *Notes* the discussion of education is peripheral and only appears because Eliot sees that our system of education is *an* important agency of cultural diffusion, and must therefore have its part in the discussion of the proper conditions of civilization. His main point is that it is a less important agency than many people believe. The discussion is by no means entirely negative; but the general effect is deflationary. In the 'Aims of Education', a series of lectures he gave at the University of Chicago in November 1950, he turned to the more positive task of setting out the exact purpose and function of formal education. The subsequently reprinted though unrevised text does not show Eliot at his best; but it does at least indicate rather more positively—though still informed by the tone of scepticism which is the characteristic hallmark of Eliot's writing—how he sees the role of education in our present society.

On Education

Eliot takes as his starting point the three aims enumerated by the late C. E. M. Joad in his book *About Education*, and already commented on in *Notes*. There these were listed as follows:

1. To enable a boy or girl to earn his or her living . . .
2. To equip him to play his part as the citizen of a democracy.
3. To enable him to develop all the latent powers and faculties of his nature and so enjoy a good life.

In the earlier book he had complained that none of these aims takes us 'very far without getting us into trouble'. Though all contained some truth, 'each of them needs to be corrected by the others'; and 'it is possible that they all need to be adjusted to other purposes as well'. The lectures on the 'Aims' were concerned with teasing out the implications of these two statements.

His first problem is the way in which the pursuit of any one of these aims may interfere with the fulfilment of one or both of the others. For instance, to learn how to earn a living is a matter of keeping in mind both the end and the means. One decides on the field of employment and then follows the proposed course of instruction; but, to develop one's latent powers, '. . . disinterestedness is necessary; you have to pursue studies for their own sake, for the love of truth, or wisdom, or at least curiosity, ignoring any practical advantages which may come to you from mastering them.' In the same way, personal self-development can very easily clash with social obligations. Hence the conclusions that

> *. . . our list of three aims of education . . . is one in which each aim is implicated with the others, and also that each one may be pursued in such a way as to interfere with the others.*[1]

[1] 'The Aims of Education', in *To Criticize the Critic* (London: Faber & Faber, 1965), p. 90.

The Aims of Education

In the course of demonstrating—at what must be termed inordinate length—the interrelatedness and yet possible disharmony of these aims, Eliot lets drop some interesting comments on the social and individual aims of education. He sees the need for social commitment; but no one can play his part in democracy who is merely adapted to its ways, for this would make him unable to foster change or make discoveries and experiments by which improvement may occur. Personal self-development on the other hand is necessarily limited by the need to earn a living as well as by the legitimate demands of the social order. In order to tease out these dilemmas, we are, in the end, driven to ask some quite fundamental philosophical, theological, ethical, and political questions; we are led, in fact, to ask profound questions about the nature of man. *En route*, we revive and expand some of the matters raised in the *Notes*. We see that there is a distinction between the good man and the good citizen, and that in order to become a good citizen it is first necessary to train the pupil to become a good man. It is accepted that democracy is the best form of government —a point to be remembered by those who accuse Eliot of possible fascist tendencies—but we are also made to appreciate that there are different sorts of democracy. Nevertheless, its essence is discovered in the fact that there is

> . . . *no* total *rule: for total rule means that somebody is in control of affairs about some of which he is totally incompetent. In a democracy, scientists and scholars and artists should rule in their own spheres: it is not a democracy when a symphony can be deviationist, or a melancholy poem about an unhappy love affair defeatist and decadent, or a biological theory subversive.*[1]

Throughout the discussion, the emphasis is to underplay the element of will. It emerges that most worthwhile aims are

[1] Ibid., p. 86.

achieved as a by-product of pursuits other than themselves. If you would educate a poet, '. . . the worst thing for him . . . would be to do nothing and care about nothing, except writing poetry.' What he chiefly needs is the pursuit of interests which will give him something to write about: 'Almost no form of knowledge comes amiss . . . because without other intellectual interests (than poetry) his experience of men and women will be very limited.' And he must be interested in these things for their own sake, not simply with a direct view to his craft. Moreover, being a good citizen does not mean merely being a well-informed citizen, one who has directly studied matters relating to public affairs. In the first place, a sense of public obligation is much better assimilated as part of the social environment of the family and relationships by which a young person gradually acquires, half unconsciously, a sense of social commitment, than it is through a programme of study involving history, government, biology, physiology, geography, and international affairs. The latter only brings the mind into play; the former is a matter of unconscious assimilation and example. Further, unless an individual is directly concerned with these matters, it is idle to expect they will have any far-reaching effect on him:

> . . . *because most of us cannot study very deeply any subject which does not concern us as individuals, which concerns us only as* members . . . *the subjects to which we can profitably give the most attention are those in which we hope to excel.*[1]

Finally, even a programme of comprehensive self-education is likely to be stillborn, in so far as it aims at nothing beyond itself: 'The pursuit of perfection, or of comprehensive culture, is not enough, because it is a by-product of our desire to do something.'

[1] Ibid., p. 90.

The Aims of Education

This is a point of major importance in considering the comparative failure of our system of education. It has too palpable a design upon us. This does not mean that we should avoid altogether the frontal attack: it does mean that such a strategy will be unlikely to succeed unless it conforms with individual predisposition or social circumstance. 'To perfect oneself, so far as one can, and in the ways in which one is perfectible, may be a duty, but only in relation to some aim beyond oneself.'

Eliot, of course, recognizes the revolutionary situation with which we are faced, that of trying to educate people who have never before been subject to formal education, and the tendency, when education is spread in this way, to impose on the rest what has been thought in the past good for the few. We are living in an age when '*construction* has priority over *growth*', when there is an inevitable drift towards standardization. But he also recognizes that we are all involved in the human situation, where what we desire often turns out to be a travesty of what we had hoped for. Thus any principle pushed to an extreme may well have side effects which had not been counted on. He analyses at greater length than in the *Notes* the current emphasis on 'equality of opportunity', and demonstrates how disastrous a rigorous application of that principle would be because it would necessitate a levelling down, for instance, so that no school would provide superior opportunities to any other. The crux of the analysis here arises out of a quotation from Simone Weil (glossed by Gustave Thibon) who points to the absurdity of the human situation—and hence, by implication, to any effort of the assertive will which does not at the same time appreciate the infinite complexity of human affairs:

The soul devoted to the pursuit of the absolutely good meets in this world with insoluble contradictions. 'Our life is impossibility, ab-

D* 99

surdity. Everything that we will is contradicted by the conditions or by the consequences attached to it. That is because we are ourselves contradiction, being merely creatures'. . . . Only imaginable goods imply no contradiction.[1]

So we are brought back to our starting point—the essential contradictions involved in trying to harmonize high level purposes which pay too little heed to the paradoxical nature of human affairs. Not only does each principle contain ambiguities and inconsistencies within itself once it is removed from the realm of the imaginary good, but each principle clashes, in some degree, with every other principle:

The ideal is a life in which one's livelihood, one's function as a citizen, and one's self-development all fit into and enhance each other. For most of us, the full pursuit of any of these aims must interfere with another . . . To get anything you want you find that you have to sacrifice something else that you want; and in getting it, you find that you have to accept other things that you do not want.[2]

Even in the midst of the essential contradictions which are inseparable from the pursuit of any ends, however, Eliot does not avoid the search for ultimate purposes. Implicit in his whole series of lectures is the realization of at once the futility and yet of the need for seeking ideal solutions; that however values may be travestied in the outcome, the search for values is nevertheless an essential concomitant of any meaningful discourse on the subject of education. Bound up with the examination of the actual, of how the notion of education has been employed in different times and in different circumstances, is a standard by which to judge such usages. Included in the question of the definition of the word 'education' is the

[1] Ibid., p. 91.
[2] Ibid., p. 104.

need for a frank recognition of its perpetually normative orientation:

> ... *we are not merely trying to say what the word education means —that is, has meant to those people ... qualified to use it—but what true education should be.*[1]

So the consideration of the meaning and significance of education leads to the point where the philosophical, ethical, and theological presuppositions have got to be brought into the open. We are led to the need to consider our doctrine of Man; and hence, in Eliot's view, to the relation of education to religion. Implicit in the value of a proper education is the notion of the 'good life'.

So we come to consider both the place of religion in education and the place of education in religion. In pursuit of the first consideration, the place of religion in education, Eliot distinguishes four possibilities:

> 1. *Where the State itself professes allegiance to a particular religion, or religious denomination, this religion may be ... taught in all the educational institutions controlled by the State.*
> 2. *The complete separation of religious instruction from instruction in other subjects. This means that in schools and colleges no religious beliefs would be taken for granted or inculcated.*
> 3. *The imparting in schools of such religious instruction as represents the common belief of the greatest part of the local society, leaving the doctrines of any particular denomination to be taught by the parents and their church. This is more or less the intention of the Education Act of 1944.*
> 4. *A mixed system, in which no religion is taught in the State schools, but in which the adherents of any religion may set up denominational schools for their own children.*

[1] Ibid., p. 121.

The first two systems are based on a principle, the latter two on expediency. Eliot finds them all unsatisfactory. The third method leads to the possibility of a new form of State Christianity: 'For the implication of teaching only a part of Christianity is that that is the only part which matters.' The fourth method negates the rightness or wrongness of either the denominational or the secular school. Clearly, both cannot be right; if the former is, then it is deplorable that so many should be deprived of its advantages; if the latter, then clearly the denominational school should be discouraged.

But we find that the first two methods are unsatisfactory also. The first encounters, in England, the fact that the nation is not homogeneous in religion, and would therefore require a dictatorial government to impose its own doctrines on society as a whole: 'For such despotism there is nothing to be said.' The second, however, is equally remiss in that

> ... *the assertion that a man's religion is his private affair, that from the point of view of society it is irrelevant, may turn out in the end to lead to a situation very favourable to the establishment of a religion, or a substitute for religion, by the State.*[1]

Once religion is weakened in the life of the community as a whole, it will become weaker in the family also:

> *Thus, when religion comes to be more and more an individual matter, and is no longer a family tie; when it becomes a matter of voluntary association on one day a week when the weather is neither too good nor too bad. . . . when it ceases to inform the whole of life; then a vacuum is discovered, and the beliefs in religion will be gradually supplanted by a belief in the State.*[2]

[1] Ibid., p. 113.
[2] Ibid., p. 114.

The Aims of Education

We thus come to see that it is not so much the place of religion in education that matters as the place of education in religion; and this because inevitably in any discussion of education—and particularly in relation to the three aims which it has been the main purpose of the lectures to discuss—concurrence can only be achieved when we have come to an agreement on ultimate problems related, for instance, to the nature of Man. Behind our discussions on education lie these ultimate questions relating to 'social and political philosophy, ethics, and finally meta-physics and theology'. Until we reach agreement on these, we shall inevitably be involved in temporary and uncertain compromises between, for instance, the claims of a community of Church or State (and, of course, of Church *and* State) and the autonomy of the individual:

> *Many a man has pursued a course which seemed folly to his family, or which appeared antisocial, or which meant pain and sacrifice for others, and we denounce him or praise him afterwards according to results which could never have been predicted.*[1]

It has to be said that such agreement is unlikely.

Eliot now pursues one further aim of education, one imposed by the nature of the times we live in, and by the need to consider claims other than those of the individual; the need, that is,

> *... to maintain the continuity of our culture—and neither continuity, nor a respect for the past, implies standing still. More than ever, we should look to education to-day to preserve us from the error of pure contemporaneity. We look to institutions of education to maintain a knowledge and understanding of the past.*[2]

[1] Ibid., p. 118.
[2] Ibid., p. 119.

103

On Education

In order to do this and preserve the wisdom of the past, 'we need to value it for its own sake, not simply defend it on the ground of its usefulness.' And this implies an education directed at those who are thus able, self-consciously, to participate in an understanding of our culture at its highest level—in Matthew Arnold's definition of culture, to be sure. Thus he repeats the implication of the *Notes*, that it may prove to be more important

> . . . *that a small number of people should be educated well, and others left with only a rudimentary education, than that everybody should be left with a share of an inferior quality of education.*[1]

This education, indeed, should be '. . . the common possession of those who have passed through the higher grades of non-specialised education'.

Eliot concludes his last lecture by referring to the difficulties that anyone who attempts to define education must inevitably encounter and which he thinks his own efforts have amply illustrated. In his attempts at definition he points to both the empirical (the attempt 'to isolate the common element in a great number of kinds of training, pursued for different ends, in very different civilisations') and the evaluative elements. He makes no bones about the fact that he has been setting out to persuade, although he adds wrily that he is not 'quite sure of what'. But, in a sense, his aim had been fulfilled if he has successfully shown the dependence of educational problems on questions which go beyond the purely educational. For in this he is certainly right. Many disputes about education are really disguised disputes about the sort of society we ought to have, or about our beliefs beyond the purely empirical, or, more vaguely still, about the ultimate

[1] Ibid., pp. 119–20.

purposes of man. They are ultimately philosophical in the old-fashioned use of the term. Although, as I indicated earlier, Eliot's exposition is often loose and over-elaborated, he does display, in a way that modern analytical philosophers might well note, the sorts of choices and ambiguities involved in the problem of definition. Often such definition may involve both lexical and prescriptive elements; and where a high level abstraction like 'education' is concerned, the prescriptive element will involve, almost unconsciously if one is not careful, a wide range of assumptions and acceptances which are disguised but not avoided behind the apparent rigour of analysis.

He concludes by urging that his main attempt has been 'to unsettle your minds', trusting that while some may agree with some of what he has said, he would be alarmed if everybody agreed: '. . . because a statement upon which everyone can agree, in the discussion of topics such as these, is pretty certain not to mean much.' Yet his search must also be admitted to involve the quest for some permanency of principle. Behind all of Eliot's work lies the search for the Absolute, together with the wisdom which admits the possibility of error. In *The Idea of a Christian Society*, for instance, he held that it would be important to have some 'settled, though not rigid agreement as to what everyone should know'; He wanted his students to be disinterested, but he thought it important for the society in which they were growing up that:

Even with a smaller amount of total information, it might have been better if they had read fewer, but the same books. In a negative liberal society you have no agreement as to there being any body of knowledge which any educated person should have acquired at any particular stage: the idea of wisdom disappears, and you get sporadic and unrelated experimentation.[1]

[1] Ibid., p. 41.

The fact is he sees, beyond pragmatism, that the teasing out of aims is not a futile exercise in face of the practicalities of the day, but is necessitated by the very nature of the exercise, cannot be left at the mercy of some high level but unexamined abstraction like 'growth' or 'development'. These considerations deserve our gratitude since such issues are so frequently avoided. The search was for '. . . permanent principles of what should be the goal of education, and permanent standards of quality in relation to which we ought to try to direct the way in which this changing world should change.' He realized that the paradox of the human condition was that such principles could never be found, but that at the same time, to be truly human was to search for them. Hence he stressed the need for implication in the voyage of discovery, yet gave carefully suggestions of checks and balances by which it would be established that no one set of findings would have a definite standing. Even in considering the relation of the secular to the religious, he saw that neither should be in a position to dominate the other:

> *We need a Church capable of conflict with the State as well as of co-operation with it. We need a Church to protect us from the State, and to define the limits of our rights, responsibilities, and duties of submission in relation to our rights, and to our responsibilities and duties to ourselves and towards God. And, owing to human fallibility, we may sometimes need the State to protect us against the Church. Too close identification can lead to oppression from which there is no escape.*[1]

Thus, any rigidities are nearly always softened by an appreciation of the other element in the equation. He was, for instance, what today would be termed subject- rather than student-centred. Thus he deprecated the way in which, fol-

[1] Ibid., p. 113.

lowing the development of the natural sciences, subject matter had proliferated, and he regretted the failure to discover 'dominant principles' which would afford some cultural cohesion to what was taught and learned. He did not consider that eighteen-year-olds were in a position to decide for themselves 'what subject or combination of subjects could best provide (them) with a liberal education'; the notion of electives, introduced to Harvard by Charles William Eliot was repugnant to T. S. Eliot, for he deplored the notion that the 'only criterion of whether a subject was necessary for your education was whether you happened at that time to be interested in it.' Yet, we recall, in his comments on Blake's education, he rejoiced in the fact that Blake had only needed to study what he wanted. This is not Mr. Facing Both-ways but an appreciation that, in such complexities, circumstances alter cases.

Conclusion

It is the difference of perspective, I have stressed, which makes Eliot so valuable a writer on education. Now that education has grown into a huge system with its own bureaucracy and vast employment potential, it has attracted its own hoard of experts, all committed to certain policies, replete with suggestions and exhortations, armed with research findings, embroiled in the day by day commerce of staff-room, lecture hall, or seminar. In the midst of all this clamour of the babel of voices and opinions, a strange silence greets the innocent visitor who raises the simple question 'What for?' The question is considered either impertinent or unanswerable, and therefore a distraction from more pressing matters. In the midst of such busyness, to ask such a question is a sign of frivolity or remoteness. Yet by their actions, all those who bustle and agitate, prevaricate or reform, constantly assume an answer to just this question. The very choice of research areas is a prey to unexpressed judgments of relevance and importance.

To have asked the question about aims, then, is an act deserving of our gratitude. But our debt to Eliot does not end here. For Eliot also provides answers which cut right across the conventional, if assumed, wisdom. It is always healthy that habits of use and wont be challenged to account for themselves especially when, paradoxically, those habits are themselves conventions of unconventionality, exhortations to the new, and therefore give an illusion of flexibility and responsiveness. But there is a rigidity of unorthodoxy as well as of received dogma; and the reaction against dogma can be as unthinking as the dogma itself. Indeed, to be alive in our present era and to be dogmatic constitutes a boldness and an orginality which in former eras was reserved for the unconventional and the iconoclastic. When all have become breakers of idols, the protector of graven images is the true revolutionary.

Now, judged by current opinion and preoccupation, Eliot's answers were unusual. This is partly because his answer to the ultimate question 'What is a man?' was also unusual. He saw constant tension as characteristic of the human situation, not harmony or adjustment. To put it another way, he saw both the horror and the glory of human life; for he believed that human existence was marked by qualitative discriminations. He was, in a word, not afraid to admit that he preferred one mode of life to another and was, therefore, prepared to judge and assess. He is typical of his age in that his judgments and assessments have about them a mildness, almost a scepticism, which readily offers the prospect of disagreement. But at least he offers something to disagree with: 'Fortunate the man who, at the right moment, meets the right friend; fortunate also the man who at the right moment meets the right enemy.' Eliot was an essentially urbane enemy; but he manifested a firm repudiation and an equally firm alternative.

He sees some simple, but to our age obscure, matters with remarkable clarity. For one thing he realizes that we cannot have everything, and that living, in addition to other things, is constantly a matter of choice. He appreciates that restriction may be creative as well as stultifying. He realizes that life is also strife and that if the struggle is worth anything it is in the direction of quality. We may—we will—disagree about what constitutes 'quality', but he has no doubt that we should seek it. He is a moralist and is not afraid of seeming so.

Hence his concern with 'culture'. To see education as a cultural manifestation is partly to see education in an anthropological context; and this is right because the content of education is just that—cultural. This content is made up of sophisticated forms of human feeling and understanding, and to see education in this way—as concerned with cultural transmission—is to see its potential in a broader and more convincing context that that implicit in most educational discussion. Here it is too often seen as a distributor, in the narrowest sense, of life chances; or as a means of implementing some social policy. To think of it as 'cultural' even in this sense is to see its possibilities of enlargement and expansiveness.

But behind the anthropologists' sense lies evaluation. The word 'culture', to Eliot, despite his concern for definition, is rarely employed in its purely descriptive sense; it nearly always has overtones of value. It is what makes life worth living. In our own days, it has suffered a decline (could what is neutral be said to decline?). It manifests itself differently in different strata of the community, and yet preserves a common likeness within the same community:

> *The culture of an artist or a philosopher is distinct from that of a mine worker or a field labourer; the culture of a poet will be somewhat different from that of a politician; but in a healthy society these are all parts of the same culture; and the artist, the poet, the philosopher, the politician, the labourer will have a culture in common, which they do not share with other people of the same occupations in other countries.*[1]

And here comes the rub. The latter belief offends against the

[1] *Notes Towards the Definition of Culture* (London: Faber & Faber, 1948), p. 120.

tenets of internationalism; the former is at variance with the beliefs of egalitarianism. As soon as one begins to think culturally, and of the culture possible in different strata of the community, one immediately realizes that equality is neither possible nor desirable. People are just not equal in either understanding or feeling.

So much might be accepted by those who stress the factor of individual difference, though this often carried the corollary of 'different but equal'. But Eliot accepts the deeper logic of his position. The differences both manifest and accentuate distinctions in society which our times try hard to cover up. The notion of 'classes', ambiguous and ill-defined though it often is, is simply an institutionalized form of these differences. This does not mean that inequalities of ability, sensibility, and moral awareness are perfectly reflected in the hierarchy of society; they are not. But the fact of such disparity makes some form of class structure essential, even if this structure is an imperfect reflection of the inherent inequalities. And these differences are perpetuated by a psychological transmission which reveals an ambiguity in the very notion of education; that the education of family is in most cases more fundamental than formal education, and that therefore, from generation to generation, there takes place a form of transmission that even the all-powerful state cannot *will* out of existence.

All this contains elements at once profound and unpalatable. In counter-attack it can perhaps be argued that even formal education can achieve more than Eliot thought it might. One is reminded of Sir Ernest Barker's confession: 'I had only my home and my school; but having my school, I had everything.' Admittedly, the school was Manchester Grammar School, and in any case, Eliot was too much the product of a formal education himself to dismiss the formal system out of hand. As a student, Eliot said he had

Conclusion

. . . a good deal of ill-regulated curiosity in out-of-the-way subjects,
who took for instance, a perverse pleasure in dabbling with late
Latin and Greek authors without having mastered the real classics.
Those who were fundamentally serious minded, and not triflers,
were able to pursue their studies for their own sake, simply because
they cared for them, . . .[1]

Nevertheless, it is clear that he saw this system might best operate not as an obligation, but as an opportunity, and then only for comparatively few. In general, he thought we try to educate too many people.

In his emphasis on the tone and pace of education, he might well be right. It is curious how very many of those who have had this notion of liberal education have emphasized that a truly liberal education must contain an element of what Aristotle called nonchalance, and Castiglione termed *sprezzatura*, effortlessness. Where Eliot is no help at all is on the education of the less able. In general he diagnosed the conditions of their industrial life well enough, if only in a brief sentence or two. He refused to blink at the fact that they were the less able and hence not capable of the same level of consciousness as their brighter companions. He saw that to hand them 'Education' as an abstraction remote from the pressures of their daily lives was but a sham and a desiccation. But then he leaves the question of what positively to do, the most serious and fundamental question facing our educational system today, and one for which there are, in an industrial society, no precedents for success. If he has anything to offer, it is simply and inadequately that they should acquire good habits; but in a world of expanded consciousness, where the people have at least the illusion of freedom and choice, this will no longer serve. For

[1] 'The Aims of Education', in *To Criticize the Critic* (London: Faber & Faber, 1965), p. 80.

the fact remains, in England at least, that there are ten precious years when something might be done, leaving some less articulate Barker with the feeling that what had been done at school had mattered.

The final impression one carries away from Eliot's social and educational theorizing combines a curious mixture of both its sense of reality and its sense of unreality. One's sense of remoteness springs from his concern for classes and Christianity as elements in the educative society. Today, Christianity is no longer a living force among the bulk of the population; and the trend of current theorizing is directly opposed to the perpetuation of anything approaching a class system, whatever the logic of events and the necessities of the social structure may impose. Furthermore, the unity that is imposed tends to be mechanical rather than organic; it stems from treating man as an abstraction. It is true that Eliot always tried to operate within a framework which he insisted was democratic, and it is true that his system of checks and balances, his appreciation that the predominance of any one power was too subject to the imperfections of human endeavour to be acceptable, produces a social system containing recognizably democratic elements. Certainly, his views are infinitely more democratic than some of those *soi-disant* democratic political ideas which serve only to disguise a collectivist totalitarianism. Of such totalitarianism there is no trace in Eliot. Nevertheless, the conscious perpetuation of a class system based, to some degree, on birth makes him seem less democratic than in fact he profoundly is; and the unity he proposes admits too freely differences in levels of consciousness to be acceptable to the unifying tendencies of the collectivist state. And so he tends to be dismissed as 'out of touch with modern realities'—and what could appear more damning than that?

Yet he draws attention to an element in the situation we,

with our different preoccupations, too frequently ignore. For, without the element of class, who is to keep up those 'superiorities' which Arnold noted as essential to a healthy culture. Eliot, in pointing to the acceptance of family continuity, may have a more accurate sense of the nature and possibilities of cultural diffusion than his opponents. There is even some slight empirical evidence to support his view. In an investigation carried out in America by Mr. H. L. Wilensky, it was found that out of a sample of 1,354 members of the community only nineteen could be found who had made 'rather heroic efforts to cultivate the best in the media'—and most of these were university professors. Mr. Wilensky's conclusion is highly significant in its support for family continuity. He finds that most of these nineteen had inherited higher occupational status than their colleagues; and he is thus led to the opinion that 'It may take rather close family supervision over more than a generation to inculcate a taste for high culture.'[1] One's observation of many first generation university students tends to bear out Mr. Wilensky's opinion.

In other ways, Eliot's sense of the realities of the human situation outweighs one's doubts about the viability in present circumstances of his social view. One gains a feeling of relief that in an age much in the grip of abstractions of only limited validity someone can face up to the profundities of human beings and of the dilemmas in which they find themselves. He plays, indeed, a vital role in that process of *un*learning which is a necessary element in any true education—an unlearning which recognizes the false hopes and promises with which we are beset and which are so often exploited for political or commercial purposes. Eliot himself surmised that 'mankind cannot bear very much reality', but he plays his part in the

---

[1] H. L. Wilensky, 'Mass Society & Mass Culture: interdependence or independence?', *American Sociological Review*, Vol. 29 (April 1964).

attempt to bring us to our senses. For one thing, he impresses on us the power and presence of history, reminding us that we are not born as abstract men and women, endowed with all the virtues and accoutrements thought proper by eighteenth-century *philosophes*, but in a particular situation of family and social circumstances, and hence subject to the pressures arising from them. Here the reality of the poetic insight informs the idealism of the social theorist; and the combination of the two enables him to see beyond the clichés of current educational acceptances. He stands as a firm indication that the educated man still has something to contribute to our thinking about education—a truth which our shrill professionals are all too ready to ignore.

Finally, he participates in a debate which has gone on now for well over a hundred years and which bears witness to one of the deepest problems of our times. It relates to a situation which is integral to our decaying moral order and can be expressed in various terms—in the conflict of individual and society, of form and content, of spontaneity and convention. What is at issue fundamentally is the relationship between an inheritance and evolving new life. So often, of course, these concepts are expressed in terms of an antagonism, as if the individual must oppose his society if he is to live, as if convention is necessarily crippling to spontaneity, as if the form must weigh heavily on the living matter, as if inheritance is an encumbrance to evolution. So we evoke 'freedom' in ways which deny fruitful order; and in reaction, we impose an order which quells a creative freedom.

It is Eliot's glory that he sees the relationship between the opposed forces in terms that appreciate both their interdependence and their mutual need for positive accommodation. His attitude to education as a social form admirably illustrates my point. He saw it as both creative and uncreative restriction, as offering both freedom and oppression in accordance with its suitability for the pupil. Hence the equivocation of his attitude toward our modern system of schooling. To some it offered possibilities of participation in the traditions of their society which was an essential concomitant to their creative achievement; to others it offered opposition with its requirement of consciousness and its insistence on an awareness beyond their capacities, or in its emphasis on the wrong sort of commitment. And so he points to the fundamental of any true education; its emphasis on a fully accepted discipline as an essential element in any worthwhile freedom. Amidst the ambiguities of the modern world, it is those who can live the experience of ambivalence who can best help our dilemmas. In this awareness of antinomy lies the supreme strength of T. S. Eliot.